Construction, Camouflage and Markings of the

Messerschmitt Me 262

By
Brett Green and Benjamin Evans
Illustrated by Thomas A. Tullis

Introduction

The Messerschmitt Me 262 *Sturmvogel*
or Stormbird, was not an especially revolutionary aircraft.

It was not the first practical jet aircraft to take to the skies. Indeed, it was not even the first twin-engine jet. Its power plants were troublesome and short-lived. The fundamental design as a low wing, stressed metal monoplane was quite conventional. Its long takeoff and landing requirements and relatively slow initial climb made it highly vulnerable to attack at these times. It was only one of a handful of jets to see service during the Second World War.

Nevertheless, the Messerschmitt Me 262 made an indelible impression on the direction of aviation.

The Stormbird was the first jet aircraft to be operationally deployed on a widespread basis. Between the days of its earliest missions in mid 1944 and the end of the Second World War, the Me 262 dramatically demonstrated the potential of the jet aircraft.

The Me 262 is perhaps best known as a single-seat fighter aircraft. Its high speed and heavy armament certainly suited the role of interceptor. However, this versatile design also proved the practicality of jets in the tasks of fighter/bomber, reconnaissance, night fighter and trainer aircraft.

The Stormbird's shark-like fuselage, swept wings and jet engines were a template for the future of military aviation.

The introduction of the Me 262 also coincided with significant changes to the instructions for painting *Luftwaffe* aircraft. The imperatives of operating from rough airfields close to the front lines, and the need to protect these precious jets on the ground, led to pragmatic field modifications to the official painting orders. Furthermore, the increasing pressure of Allied bombing created a chaotic production environment where many aircraft components were delivered partially painted or completely unpainted.

All of these circumstances combined to demonstrate a very diverse range of finishes on the Me 262 despite its short service history.

This book touches on some technical and operational issues, but the main focus is on the colors and markings of this jet pioneer. A range of camouflage schemes and markings are displayed in wartime photographs and color profiles. The Stormbird Colors are examined in great detail on the last surviving example of an Me 262A2a with elements of its original paintwork intact.

The full range of colors and markings used on the Messerschmitt Me 262 may never be revealed, but we hope that *Stormbird Colors* will provide some insight into this fascinating subject.

Acknowledgements

Stormbird Colors is the product of an enthusiastic team effort.

Jerry and Judy Crandall of Eagle Editions perform a much broader role than simple publisher. Jerry has cheerfully put up with many long telephone conversations across international time zones and a barrage of email correspondence over the last year. His innovative suggestions, perceptive feedback and deep insight into *Luftwaffe* matters are a constant inspiration. Judy has also played an active role with her contribution to formatting and keeping the team focused.

The authors are also delighted to have Tom Tullis' beautiful color profiles in this book. Tom has been another lively participant in the team with an input to interpretation of colors and markings.

The remarkable photo collection of Jim Crow has been the source for many of the photographs in this book. The authors are very grateful for Jim's enthusiasm for our project, and his proactive hunt through his vast collection for appropriate material.

Thanks are also due to Robert Bracken, Bill Harper, Cecil Mann and Alan Scheckenbach for access to important photos and information.

Ben Evans would like to thank his erstwhile colleagues at the Australian War Memorial, in particular David Pearson, John White, David Crotty, John Kemister, Ian Hodges and Katy Parr, all of whom either advised on, or put up with enthused ramblings about, *Luftwaffe* aircraft.

Thanks are also due Werner Hermann, JG 53 pilot, whose evocative descriptions of the skies over Germany in 1945 have given Ben a much deeper understanding of what motivated *Luftwaffe* pilots in the face of overwhelming USAAF might.

Last, but by no means least, Ben would like to thank Wendy, whose bemused tolerance of his *Luftwaffe* addiction, and associated book buying habits, is nothing if not remarkable!

Brett Green would like to thank his long-suffering family. His wife Debra has once again shouldered the extra burden with the household and children, Charlotte and Sebastian, while this book was being written.

In conclusion, the authors encourage anyone with information or photographs that will further enhance our understanding of this chaotic subject to contact me via the publisher, Eagle Editions Ltd, eagle@eagle-editions.com, or at my email address bgreen@bigpond.com

The publishers wish to personally thank James Crow, the late Lorenze Rasse, Todd Rasse, Günther Sengfelder, and Dave Wadman for their assistance in providing materials for this publication.

Color Notes

Color interpretation from Black and White photographs amounts to educated guesswork, at the very best. The advent of computer technology has greatly aided in this endeavor. The computer has, through grayscale comparison and analysis, eliminated much guesswork from the evaluation of true colors.

ISBN: 0966070690

Library of Congress Catalog Number 2002105721

First Edition

Copyright © 2002 Eagle Editions Ltd.

Printed in Korea

Layout and graphic design by Kent Haaven, *Images*, Scottsdale AZ

Library of Eagles

Eagle Editions Ltd.
Post Office Box 580
Hamilton MT 59840 USA
www.eagle-editions.com

We are interested in hearing from those who may have photographic or data material for use in future publications.

Contents

Introduction..2

Acknowledgements..3

Color Notes..4

Authors' Biographical Notes..6

Development of the Messerschmitt Me 262....................................7

Prototype and Pre-Production Series Me 262 jet fighters...............10

The Jumo 109-004B Turbojet...12

Stormbird Colors...13

The Story of "Black X"...38

Camouflage and Markings of "Black X".......................................44

Parts Manual Diagrams..46

Colors on "Black X"...48

"Black X" General Paint Features; Color Photo Essay..................49

Me 262 Color Profiles..74

Me 262 Color Profile Notes..78

Me 262 Photographs From Film...80

Me 262 Technical Illustrations..81

Werknummer Data Plate Locations..84

Scale Drawings in 1/48 scale..86

References...87

Addendum to *"Augsburg's Last Eagles"* - EF #3........................88

Authors'
Biographical Notes

Benjamin Evans

Ben Evans, an archaeologist by training, has maintained a long fascination for German aircraft of the Second World War.

He had the privilege of working for the Australian War Memorial for several years, which served to encourage this interest. As a staff member of the Memorial, Ben contributed a number of articles to the magazine *Wartime* on a variety of military history topics.

Ben lives in Canberra, Australia with his wife Wendy and two Belgian Shepherd dogs, and works in the Australian Public Service.

Brett Green

Brett Green lives in Sydney, Australia with his wife Debbie and two children.

An early fascination with aviation history created a thirst for research and building model aircraft. This enthusiasm spawned regular articles and reviews for a number of magazines including Aviation in Miniature, IPMS News and Views, and Australian Models and Hobbies.

In March 1998, Brett launched the online magazine Hyperscale (www.hyperscale.com), a popular website catering to the historian, modeler and researcher with reviews, articles and interactive discussion groups.

Brett is also the author of *Augsburg's Last Eagles*, published by Eagle Editions in 2001.

Development of the
Messerschmitt Me 262

The development of the Messerschmitt Me 262 was closely linked to the evolution of turbojet engines by German manufacturers during the late 1930s. Throughout its short career, the Stormbird's effectiveness was defined by the capabilities of its engines.

Messerschmitt began design studies for a jet fighter in 1938. Having interested *Luftwaffe* technical officers, an order was placed for three prototypes using BMW P3302 turbojet in March 1940. The official designation "Me 262" was allocated at the same time.

The airframe was developed rapidly thanks to the experience of the Messerschmitt design team. By 1941, work on the airframe far surpassed the development of the BMW engines.

To allow testing of the airframe to go proceed without the BMW engines, a *Jumo* 210G piston engine was installed in the nose of Me 262 V1. It made its first flight from Augsburg on 17 April 1941. Fritz Wendel was the test pilot. This first prototype provided the Messerschmitt design team with low-speed flight handling data and the aircraft was returned to the hanger to await its jet engines. This took almost a year.

On 25 March 1942, with Wendel once again at the controls, Me 262 V1 took off under the power of three engines. The new BMW engines flamed out almost immediately upon getting airborne. Wendel limped back to the airfield on the single piston engine. The problem was blamed on turbulence from the propeller of the piston engine entering the jet intakes, breaking away several compressor blades. Even allowing for this external factor in the failure of the BMW jet, its compressor layout needed major redesign and BMW played no further part in the development of the Me 262.

Messerschmitt Me 262 V3, radio code PC+UC, photographed prior to its first flight on 18 July 1942. A Messerschmitt Me 321 "Gigant" dominates the background.

By chance, the *Jumo* 109-004A turbojet was cleared for flight testing shortly after V1's near-disastrous flight. The *Jumo* turbojet offered almost twice the power of the BMW units. Me 262 V3 was redesigned to accept the *Jumo* jet engines. The piston engine was not installed on this prototype in order to avoid the turbulence problems suffered on V1's test flight. On 18 July 1942 Wendel made the first test Me 262 flight on jet power alone from the Messerschmitt company airfield at Leipheim in Bavaria.

The Me 262 was still generally regarded as a novel experiment by senior *Luftwaffe* officers even as the prototype was building up flying hours. Their attention was firmly fixed on the rough airstrips deep in the Soviet Union, where the long runways and constant maintenance required by a jet fighter would be a costly liability. In 1942 the Messerschmitt Bf 109 and the Focke-Wulf Fw 190 were more than capable of handling their opponents. Despite these official reservations, 15 pre-production Me 262 jets were ordered after V3's July 1942 flight. The order was increased to 30 Me 262s in October of the same year.

The *Luftwaffe*'s circumstances had changed dramatically by the first half of 1943. USAAF bombers were hitting targets in Germany in broad daylight and the *Luftwaffe* was forced onto the defensive across all fronts. The requirement for a high performance interceptor was now clear. The Messerschmitt Me 262 was the obvious choice to fill this role.

The Me 262 was therefore ordered into production on the optimistic assumption that problems with the *Jumo* problems would be solved quickly. Series production was planned to commence in January 1944, with full production starting in February and reaching 60 aircraft a month in May.

Having met this schedule, the first pre-production Me 262A-0 jets were deployed to *Erprobungskommando* 262 at Lechfeld, Bavaria, in early 1944 for service testing. Perhaps the most important finding made by this unit was that the Me 262 was unforgiving to inexperienced pilots.

As the *Erprobungskommando* 262 continued its test flight program during May 1944, Hitler intervened in the Me 262's development. In a moment of lucidity he understood two important facts. First, the coming Allied invasion of Europe could only be repelled on the beaches and second, Allied air superiority over the landings would be such that only a very fast bomber would be able to get through. Hitler was buoyed by Messerchmitt's assurances that the Me 262 could carry bombs and irritated by the vacillation of Göring and Milch on the issue. On 23 May 1944, he decreed that all further Me 262 production must be assigned exclusively to a Stormbird bomber. Production of the pure fighter variant ceased. The first Me 262 bombers were delivered to KG 51 on 20 June 1944.

By June 1944, *Erprobungskommando* 262 had 15 jet fighters at its disposal, all early production aircraft that could not be modified to carry bombs. Occasional interception missions were flown against high-flying Allied reconnaissance aircraft, with limited success. In August, *Major* Walter Nowotny assumed command of *Erprobungskommando* 262 and it was renamed *Kommando Nowotny*.

Development continued on the Me 262 and, in particular, its *Jumo* engines. By September 1944 a series of incremental improvements had increased the expected service life of the *Jumo* engines to 25 hours. The design was then frozen to allow series production. In the same month Hitler rescinded his "bomber only" order and *Kommando* Nowotny, with 23 aircraft, was declared ready for frontline service. It moved to airfields at Achmer and Hesepe. Despite Hitler's "bomber only" order, the entry into service of the Me 262 as a fighter was probably delayed by only a month.

The *Jumo* engines continued to be plagued by reliability problems right up to the end of the war. Nevertheless, the Messerschmitt Me 262 held the distinction of being the first jet fighter to see active service and its contribution to post-war aircraft designs was immense.

However, in common with other advanced German technology of the Second World War, it was too little, too late.

W.Nr.	Type	Pilots	Details	Fate
26200 001 PC+UA	262 V1	Fritz Wendel, Karl Baur, Lukas Schmid	One *Jumo* 210 G (*W. Nr.* 42012), two-bladed VDM Type 9-110 propeller. Later equipped with two BMW P3302, then two *Jumo* 004 A jet engines.	
26200 002 PC+UB	262 V2	Willi Ostertag		Crashed fatally, 18 April 1943, on aircraft's 48th flight. Caused by a malfunctioning tailplane incidence mechanism.
26200 003 PC+UC	262 V3	Fritz Wendel	Two *Jumo* 109-004 A (TL) engines. First to fly on pure jet power, 18 July 1942.	
26200 004 PC+UD	262 V4	Fritz Wendel, Adolf Galland (22 May 1943)	Two *Jumo* 004 A jet engines	Crashed on take-off at Schkeuditz on its 51st flight, 26 July 1943.
26200 005 PC+UE	262 V5	*Hptm* Werner Thierfelder	First aircraft with tricycle undercarriage. Two *Jumo* 004 A-0 jet engines and two Borsig RI-502 take-off assistance rockets.	Aircraft crashed for the second time due to nosewheel tire blowout, 1 February 1944. Not repaired by war's end.
130001 VI+AA	262 V6	Kurt Schmidt	Two *Jumo* 004 B-0 jet engines.	Crashed on 28th flight, 9 March 1945.
130002 VI+AB	262 V7	*Uffz.* Hans Flachs	Two *Jumo* 004 B-1 jet engines, clear view canopy and pressurized cockpit.	Crashed fatally on its 31st flight, Lechfeld, 19 May 1944.
130003 VI+AC	262 V8		Tests armament of four RB MK 108 cannon. Later used in active service.	
130004 VI+AD	262 V9		Used in electro-acoustical homing tests prior to being modified into HG I high performance test bed.	Abandoned at Lechfeld, 1945
130005 VI+AE	262 V10		Last of the prototype series, and the first modified for fighter-bomber testing. Later used in experiments with towed bombs.	
130006 VI+AF	262 S1			

Table 1: Prototype and Pre-Production Series Me 262 jet fighters

W. Nr.	Type	Pilots	Details	Fate
130 007 VI+AG	262 S2	Hans Herlitzius	First of the Leipheim production series. Due to prototype losses, retained for test purposes. Exceeded 1,000 km/h.	
130008 VI+AH	262 S3		First flew 16 April 1944. Active service from May 1944.	
130008 VI+AG	262 V-12	*Ofw.* Becker	Almost certainly the same aircraft as above with its registration transposed from *W. Nr.* 130007	Crashed on a training flight from Lechfeld, 16 June 1944. Pilot badly injured.
130009 VI+AI	262 S4		First flew 5 May 1944. On active service from that month.	
130010 VI+AJ	262 S5		Sent to Blohm und Vos*s* for conversion to a two-seater.	Crashed on landing on its 47th flight, 8 October 1944.
130011 VI+AK	262 S6	*Hptm.* Theirfelder	First flew April 1944.	Crashed fatally on 18 July 1944 due to separation of turbine strator rings.
130012 VI+AL	262 S7		First flew May 1944	
130013 VI+AM	262 S8		First flew May 1944	Destroyed in an air raid, 19 July 1944.
130014 VI+AN	262 S9		First flew May 1944.	
130015 VI+AO	262 S10		First flew May 1944.	Survived to at least 26 April 1945, when it is recorded as with JV 44, but finally found abandoned at Lechfeld, war's end.
130016 VI+AP	262 S11		First flew May 1944.	
130017 VI+AQ	262 S12	*Lt.* Alfred Schreiber	First 262 to engage an enemy aircraft, a 544 Sqn. Mosquito, 26 July 1944.	Broken up October 1944.
130018 VI+AR	262 S13		First flew June 1944.	Broken up October 1944.
130019 VI+AS	262 S14		First flew June 1944.	
130020 VI+AT	262 S15		First flew June 1944.	Damaged January 1945.

Table 1: Prototype and Pre-Production Series Me 262 jet fighters

The
Jumo 109-004B Turbojet

The *Jumo* 109-004B turbojet was both a crucial asset and a disappointing liability for the Messerschmitt Me 262. The Stormbird's jet powerplant was technically advanced but it was also temperamental in service. Each engine had a very short life before parts started to wear out.

The spine of the engine was a complex aluminum casting. It supported the compressor (with 25 bolts), the combustion chambers and the turbine, as well as providing the three mountings that attached the engine to the wing.

Unlike many of its contemporaries, the *Jumo* engine was an axial flow design. This means that the air taken into the engine was compressed down the axis of the engine rather than out to the combustion chambers as in the centrifugal flow British units. This enabled the use of a multi-stage compressor, which in turn allowed the airflow to be used for other tasks in the *Jumo* units, an integral part of the engine's design. Air was bled from stages 3 and 5 to cool the 6 combustion chambers, while air from the final stage, stage 8, was used to cool the turbine. German materials technology was not capable of manufacturing parts that could withstand very high operating temperatures, most notably in the single stage turbine, so this emphasis on cooling was an essential requirement. However, this sophisticated cooling mechanism came at a cost. A post-war American analysis estimated that drawing air off the compressor resulted in a 7% loss of potential power.

The turbine was built in two forms. Each had 61 blades. The first type used solid blades made from hardened chrome steel, comprising 30% nickel, 14% chrome, 1.75% titanium and 0.12% carbon. Later turbines used hollow blades (made from the same material), apparently only as a weight and material saving measure since, in terms of labor, 15 separate operations were required to manufacture each hollow blade. Furthermore, the hollow blades were not an operational success as their trailing edges tended to come apart, sometimes resulting in catastrophic failure of the turbine. Very late model turbines had two rivets in the blade's trailing edges to prevent this.

The thrust produced by the engine could be adjusted by up to 25% using a moveable bullet in the aft of the engine. This was the primary engine control in flight, as the engine was very sensitive to throttle adjustments. In early *Jumo* units, the bullet's setting was manipulated by the pilot, but in the later engines was slaved to the throttle controls in order to improve thrust control.

The *Jumo* 109-004 turbo jet was extremely advanced technically, but this innovation was not matched by endurance. The *Jumo* 109-004 had an average operational life expectancy of only 10-12 hours. Notably, the Jumos used in Arado Ar 234 bombers lasted longer because their operational profile required less frequent alterations to throttle settings during flight.

The limitations of wartime German materials technology let down an otherwise sound design. At war's end, experimental high-temperature alloys enabled a *Jumo* on a test stand to reach 500 hours use, with 150 hours expected in service. The way forward for turbo jet design was clear.

German Jet Colors – 1944-45
Stormbird Colors

The *Reichsluftfahrtministerium*, or RLM, supervised the operations and administration of Germany's burgeoning military aviation capability from April 1933 until the end of the Second World War.

The *Luftwaffe* was formally unveiled in March 1935 but the RLM remained the administration authority for many functions including establishing and maintaining paint standards.

Written instructions and color chips were supplied to all aircraft factories to ensure astandard appearance. These instructions were strictly observed until mid-1944 with few exceptions.

The versatile Messerschmitt Me 262 straddled several roles including day fighter, night fighter, bomber and reconnaissance aircraft. During its prototype phase, the Me 262 was subject to these mid-war camouflage instructions issued in November 1941. Early prototypes wore colors that were applicable to their planned operational role.

The first fighter prototypes were therefore finished in the mid-war scheme of RLM 74 Gray-Green and RLM 75 Gray-Violet upper surfaces. These colors were combined with RLM 02 Gray for a mottle on the fuselage sides. Lower surfaces were painted RLM 76 Light Blue.

By July 1944 a small number of Messerschmitt Me 262 fighters had already entered service with *Erprobungskommando 262*, later renamed *Kommando Nowotny,* and *Kommando Schenk*. It appears likely that some of these early operational Stormbirds also wore the official mid-war scheme of RLM 74 Gray-Green and RLM 75 Gray-Violet on the upper surfaces.

Different paint finishes were specified for specific aircraft roles. In November 1941, the RLM issued a comprehensive document that formalized colors and camouflage schemes. The colors can be summarized as follows:

Aircraft Type	Camouflage Finish
Day Fighters & Heavy Fighters	Colors 74 Gray-Green & 75 Gray-Violet - Upper surfaces Colors 74 Gray-Green, 75 Gray-Violet & 02 Gray - Mottle finish on fuselage sides Color 76 Light Blue - Lower surfaces
Bombers & Transports	Colors 70 Black-Green & 71 Dark Green – Upper surfaces and fuselage sides Color 65 Light Blue – Lower surfaces
Maritime Aircraft	Colors 72 Green & 73 Green – Upper surfaces Color 65 Light Blue – Lower surfaces
Tropical Aircraft	Colors 79 Sand-Yellow & 80 Olive-Green – Upper surfaces Color 78 Light Blue – Lower surfaces
Trainers	Any appropriate color except Silver

Messerschmitt Me 262 V3, coded PC+UC, at Leipheim, Germany on 18 July 1942 prior to its first flight.

This prototype displays the classic mid-war color scheme of RLM 74 Gray-Green and 75 Gray-Violet upper surfaces with RLM 76 lower surfaces.

The wing upper surface wears a splinter camouflage of RLM 74 Gray-Green and RLM 75 Gray-Violet with a soft demarcation. Lower surfaces are painted RLM 76 Light Blue. The fuselage sides display a heavy and regular mottle of RLM 74, RLM 75 and RLM 02.

The different shape of the rear of the engine nacelle is obvious in this view.

The framed canopy is also of interest.

Browns and Greens

A number of Messerschmitt Me 262 prototypes were dedicated bomber or anti-tank variants. It appears more than likely that these prototypes were finished in the standard bomber scheme of the day – RLM 70 Black-Green and RLM 71 Dark Green upper surfaces with lower surfaces in RLM 65 Light Blue.

Messerschmitt Me 262 V11, werknummer 110555, was converted in February 1945 as the second prototype Me 262A-2a Fast Bomber with the Lotfe gunsight. This variant was intended to vastly improve the bombing accuracy of the Stormbird. The unarmed Me 262 V11 featured a clear nose. As a dedicated bomber variant, it is possible that this aircraft was finished in RLM 70 Black-Green and RLM 71 Dark Green.

The camouflage wraps around the leading edge of the wing with an irregular scalloped demarcation underneath. The Light Blue on the engine nacelle appears to have been sprayed over the darker camouflage colors. Also note the pale vertical stripes along panel joins on the front and rear fuselage.

This Stormbird was also possibly finished in RLM 70 and RLM 71 upper surfaces. Messerschmitt Me 262A-1a/U4 W. Nr. 170083, photographed at Lechfeld Germany during May 1945. This variant is fitted with a 50 mm cannon.

Defensive Colors

The *Luftwaffe* was fighting a desperate defensive war by 1944. The skies of northern Europe were dominated by Allied fighters and bombers, and the *Luftwaffe* was acutely short of fuel and experienced aircrew.

The mid-war Gray camouflage scheme for *Luftwaffe* fighters was required for effective camouflage over the English Channel and against the cloudy skies of northern Europe. The emphasis had now shifted to protecting aircraft on the ground. This was a particularly high priority for the Messerschmitt Me 262 owing to its high strategic value and its vulnerability during its long take-offs and landings.

On 1 July 1944 the RLM issued a document (GL/C-10 IV E) containing reference to a new issue of Brown and Green colors 81, 82 and 83. These colors represented a more appropriate method to conceal aircraft from aerial attack.

Initially, RLM 81 and 82 were to replace RLM 70 and 71 on bombers and reconnaissance aircraft. Where existing stocks of the old colors existed, color 82 could be used in combination with color 70; or color 81 could be used with color 71. By mid-1944, this scheme officially applied to bombers, transports and some trainers.

No color chips were supplied to factories, and descriptive labels were sometimes ambiguous. These factors then led to a very non-standard appearance to colors 81 and 82. RLM 81 has been observed in shades from Dark Olive Green to Brown-Violet, and even to a washed-out Pinkish Tan similar to heavily weathered US Air Force Olive Drab. RLM 82 sometimes appeared as a Bright, Light Green, and other times as a darker shade. Some of these discrepancies may have been the result of field mixed paints, but variations in application and heavy weathering clearly took toll of the intended shade.

"White 4", werknummer 500226 of JG 7 at Ebendorf in Germany during May 1945.

This aircraft displays one of the standard color schemes for the Messerschmitt Me 262. Upper surfaces are finished in a segmented scheme of RLM 81 Brown-Violet and RLM 82 Light Green. Lower surfaces are painted RLM 76 Light Blue. The fuselage demarcation line is very low, and the delineation of the wing leading is a tight scallop. The JG 7 RV (Reichsverteidigung, or Reich Defense) band on the rear fuselage can also be seen in this photo. The band is RLM 24 Dark Blue (front) and RLM 23 Red (rear). Fuselage cross is White, and the tail Hakenkreuz is solid Black.

The same documents describe a third color, 83 Dark Green. This color was frequently used to replace color 74 on fighter aircraft from mid-1944.

By August 1944 at least two RLM orders noted the withdrawal of color 74 Gray-Green. This was to be replaced with color 83 Dark Green. The default fighter camouflage scheme was therefore colors 75 Gray-Violet and 83 Dark Green on the upper surfaces and color 76 Light Blue on the lower surfaces.

Despite this scheme being widely applied to other fighter types including the Messerschmitt Bf 109 and Focke-Wulf Fw 190, the 75/83 camouflage was observed relatively infrequently on the Messerschmitt Me 262. It was much more common to see the Stormbird finished in the late-war Browns and Greens.

Messerschmitt Me 262A-1a werkummer 500075 or 500079, "F1+DA" photographed at Giebelstadt Germany in April 1945. This fascinating Stormbird is finished in a low contrast, squiggly application of RLM 81 Brown-Violet and RLM 83 Dark Green over RLM 76 lower surfaces. The line of spots dividing the colors of the upper and lower fuselage is of particular interest.

The nose cap and fin tip are painted Red, separated from the camouflage finish by a narrow White line. The rim of the jet intakes are also painted Red.

The nose gear door is marked with the letter "D" followed by a tiny letter "A". Both letters appear to be painted in Black. Also note that the forward gear strut appears to be very dark. The color looks more like RLM 66 Black Gray than the specified RLM 02 Gray.

According to the standard Luftwaffe bomber identification scheme, "F1" indicates KG 76, "D" is the individual letter for the fourth aircraft in the Staffel and "A" represents the Geschwaderstab Flight. The individual letter of staff aircraft would normally be painted Green or Blue. The combination of this Geschwaderstab Flight identification with the Red markings is surprising, as Red markings are usually associated with II. Gruppe. These Red markings may therefore be the remnants of former service with KG(J) 54. Although this aircraft is attached to a bomber unit, the external bomb racks are not fitted.

The tail Hakenkreuz appears to be solid Black, the fuselage Balkenkreuz is the White outline type, and lower wing crosses are White outline with a Black center.

The wings and horizontal tailplanes are probably painted in a standard segmented scheme of 81/82. The leading edge of the wings displays a tight, wavy demarcation between upper and lower surfaces. Upper wing crosses are almost certainly the White outline style.

Unidentified Messerschmitt Me 262 photographed at Erfurt, Germany during April 1945. The very low contrast between the two upper surface colors suggests RLM 81 Brown-Violet and RLM 83 Dark Green with a sporadic mottle in these two colors below the mid-fuselage demarcation. Lower surfaces are RLM 76 Light Blue.

Another unidentified Messerschmitt Me 262 photographed at Erfurt, Germany during April 1945. The thin application of camouflage colors is indicated by the very obvious vertical lines on the fuselage. These lines are most likely Dark Gray putty used to seal the gaps between fuselage panels. The fuselage appears to be finished in RLM 82 Light Green with a mottle of RLM 81 Brown-Violet.

The upper rear of the fuselage seems to have received a solid application of the darker color (RLM 81). The wings are probably a standard pattern of RLM 81 Brown-Violet and RLM 82 Light Green. Note the sharp demarcation between these two colors on the inboard port side flap.

Messerschmitt Me 262 V2, werknummer 170056, photographed at Lechfeld, Germany in 1946.

This Stormbird was abandoned after the nose gear collapsed on landing. Werknummer 170056 was a flying
test bed for elements of the proposed two-seater Me
262B-2a night fighter.

The fin installed on the fuselage spine behind the cockpit
was intended to assess the aerodynamic impact of the
longer canopy required for the two-seater. The aircraft is
equipped with both FuG 218 Neptun radar on the nose,
and FuG 226 vertical radar dipoles on the wings.

Werknummer 170056 was substantially repainted after

initial testing of the Neptun radar. By war's end, the aircraft displayed large patches of a light color, possibly
RLM 82 Light Green, over its original dark Green finish.
A very dark color is also present on the mid fuselage near
the rear of the canopy. Lower surfaces are painted RLM
76 Light Blue. A strip of bare metal can be seen between
the steel nose and the alloy mid fuselage. The engine
intake is also unpainted.

Although it is not visible in this view, the nose cap is
painted a very dark color - probably RLM 70 Black
Green. The Hakenkreuz is low-visibility White outline, as
is the fuselage Hakenkreuz. The werknummer is stenciled in Black, and lower wing crosses are applied in
Black and White.

Opposite page; Messerschmitt Me 262, W. Nr. 111755,
photographed on 17 June, 1945 at Echterdingen in
Germany. This aircraft wears a simple finish similar to
others in the same werknummer block.

The fuselage sides appear to be painted in a thin, overall
coat of either RLM 82 Light Green. The leading edge of
the tail was constructed of wood, and the dark primer
may be seen below the thin top coat.

The top of the horizontal tail exhibits a sharp demarcation between RLM 81 Brown-Violet and RLM 82 Light
Green.

The stencil-style werknummer, the slightly misaligned
Black and White Hakenkreuz and the solid mass balance
on the leading edge of the deflected starboard elevator
are of interest. This aircraft was later sent to Wright
Field in the United States for flight testing.

Two views Messerschmitt Me 262A-1 werknummer 110376 photographed at Neubiberg, Germany in 1945. "White 7" of III./EJG 2 exhibits a solid, dark finish with a scribbly mottle on the lower nose.

The low contrast between the upper surface colors suggests that they may be RLM 81 Brown-Violet and RLM 83 Dark Green. The hard-edged dapple pattern on the fin and rudder is RLM 83 Dark Green over a very pale version of RLM 76 Light Blue.

Compare this color to the RLM 76 on the sides of the engine nacelle. This pattern is applied with a stencil. The dapple pattern tail was commonly seen on the Stormbirds of Kommando Nowotny.

Although the front of the photograph is heavily blurred, the nose cap appears to be unpainted.

The same aircraft, werknummer 110376, on a scrapheap in December 1945 at Neubiberg. Note the very unusual White Hakenkreuz with a fine Black outline, the dapple pattern on the rear fuselage spine and the unpainted wing leading edge.

Three Me 262s of III./KG(J) 54: on the left with the wavy White overpainted lines, is a Me 262 A-2a bomber version, the other two aircraft appear to be standard Me 262 A-1a fighters (Jabos). Of interest are the three distinctive camouflage patterns on these aircraft. March 1945, Neuberg near Frankfurt, Germany

Two views of Messerschmitt Me 262A, werknummer 500531, was photographed at Linz, Austria during 1945. The "chessboard" mottle is of particular interest. Also note the scalloped demarcation just visible on the leading edge of the starboard wing. The solid base color is proba-

bly RLM 82 Light Green, while the mottle is either RLM 81 Brown-Violet or RLM 83 Dark Green. The unusual pattern on the starboard engine nacelle is the result of a small fire. The X marking on the bottom of the rudder is probably an inspection mark applied after capture.

Variations

The chaotic late-war situation inevitably led to a breakdown of standardization.

Evidence of this breakdown may be seen by the use of primer and marking colors as camouflage; and the widespread appearance of totally undocumented colors on the lower surfaces of Messerschmitt Bf 109s and Focke-Wulf Fw 190s. These colors ranged from Blue-Gray to Yellow-Green. It is not yet known if these colors were standard but undocumented colors; or improvised field and factory mixes.

There is little evidence that these late-war "Sky" colors were used on the Messerschmitt Me 262, however significant variations in standard colors were observed on Stormbirds. For example, RLM 76 Light Blue varied in shade from a light Blue-Gray color to a very pale Blue.

During the Allies march across Europe, Messerschmitt Me 262s were also frequently found in operational condition but unpainted. It appears that this valuable weapon was rushed to front-line units with the barest minimum of protective finishes applied to steel components and to panel joins.

Messerschmitt Me 262 S7, V1 + AL. werknummer 130012 "Red 6" of
Erprobungskommando Thierfelder *photographed in April or May 1944.*

Me 262 S3 werknummer 130008 "Red 3" also of **Erprobungskommando Thierfelder,** *after nose gear collapse on 16 April 1944. Both these aircraft were finished in overall RLM 76 Light Blue. Radio codes appeared on the fuselage sides and wing undersurfaces in Black. The individual aircraft numbers were carried on the nose in Red. The style of the single digit "6" on the aircraft above is quite unusual.*

Here is Messerschmitt Me 262A-1a werknummer *111711*. This aircraft was assembled at Hessental by Autobedarf Schwabisch Hall. It was surrendered on 31 March 1945 by Messerschmitt test pilot Hans Hay at Frankfurt/Rhein-Main after its first test flight.

This aircraft wears only primer and filler. The fuselage and wings have been left in their natural alloy color. Even the steel nose of this example remains unpainted. The steel engine nacelles are primed, but the intakes are polished natural metal.

It is likely that the cannon access panel is painted RLM 02 Gray, and the radio access hatch (under the fuselage Hakenkreuz) is an unidentified pale color – perhaps a cream-colored primer. Panel joints have been filled and smoothed with putties of various colors, mostly Gray.

The cannon ports have also been roughly filled, although this is more likely to have taken place after capture.

The "last three" of the **werknummer**, *711*, is stencilled on the fin. This number is repeated in tiny digits on the rear fuselage near the base of the fin as an aid for assembly of components.

The simplified Black fuselage markings are to be expected. The upper wing crosses, not visible in the view, are applied in the Black outline style. However, it is surprising to see earlier-style Black and White underwing crosses on this hastily finished Stormbird.

Werknummer *111711 was forwarded to Wright Field in the USA where it was flown on twelve occasions before crashing on 20 August 1946.*

W. Nr. 111712 from the same production batch as W. Nr. 111711. The finish and markings are almost identical with the exception of the rudder. The whole rudder assembly appears to be finished in Red primer. The last three numbers of the werknummer, 712, are stenciled in small digits on the rear fuselage. The number "56" painted in tiny type on the empennage under the stabilizer, and inside the lower "hook" of the tail Hakenkreuz.

A discussion is taking place between personnel of III./KG(J) 54 in front of a Me 262 A-2a with distinctive White wavy lines sprayed over the basic camouflage used by this unit. Note the tread on the tire and the lack of scissors link on the landing gear leg. Also of interest is the uniforms worn by the pilots: the pilot on the left is wearing a leather flying helmet with the net top, type L Kp N 101 with the uncommon Light Brown ear pieces. Note the variations in the colors of leather which could be Gray Green, or Gray Blue combinations. March 1945, Neuberg near Frankfurt, Germany

On this page, two images of Messerschmitt Me 262, W. Nr. 110506, photographed in northern Germany after discovery by Canadian forces. This aircraft is possibly finished in bomber colors RLM 65 Light Blue with a "squiggle" camouflage pattern of RLM 70 Black-Green and RLM 71 Dark Green on the upper surfaces of the wings and the fuselage. It is also possible that this low contrast scheme comprises the late-war colors RLM 81 Brown-Violet and RLM 83 Dark Green, or even a combination of the old and new colors.

In the picture to the left, it is interesting to note that the upper wing Balkenkreuz has been slightly over-sprayed by the dark camouflage colors. This suggests that the aircraft may have been originally delivered in overall Light Blue, with the darker colors being applied at unit level.

This is probably Me 262 A-1a/U3 of 2./NAGr. 6, or Me 262 A-4a, "White 33", W. Nr. 500539, at Lechfeld, Germany in 1945. This reconnaissance variant is also probably finished in a combination of Greens.   Note Me 262 V9 (VI + AD) to the right of "White 33".

Messerschmitt Me 262 V9 (VI + AD) werknummer 130004 at the same location from a different angle. Werknummer 130004 was one of the original Messerschmitt Me 262A prototypes. It still wears its mid-war, all-Gray finish. The entire mid-fuselage has been painted Black. This was not a camouflage meas-ure, but was probably intended as a stark contrast for White wool tufts used to determine the aerodynamic qualities of the airframe. During its career, V9 was used in electro-acoustical homing tests prior to being modified into HG I high performance test bed.

Markings

The Messerschmitt Me 262 shared many late-war markings in common with its contemporary *Luftwaffe* fighters, bombers and reconnaissance aircraft. These included colored fuselage bands and unit-specific RV (*Reichsverteidigung*, or *Reich* Defense) bands.

RV bands were colorful rings around the rear fuselage of fighter aircraft designed to assist German flak units, ground troops and other fighter pilots to identify friendly aircraft. An order was issued in February 1945 that all fighter aircraft were to wear these colors, formalizing a common practice on the Western Front since mid-1944. Owing to more pressing issues, the order was only sporadically observed in Me 262 units.

Many Stormbirds also displayed other distinctive plumage. *Staffel* colors were sometimes painted on the tip of the fin, or the nose cone, or on the engine intakes. Individual aircraft numbers could appear in the conventional position on the rear fuselage but also frequently appeared on the forward fuselage. Certain units adopted characteristic fuselage markings such as diagonal stripes or badges.

Messerschmitt Me 262A-1a, W. Nr. 501232 "Yellow 5", photographed at München-Riem airfield in Germany during 1945. This aircraft was formerly attached to I./KG (J) 54.

The Red and Black checkered tailband is a particularly interesting marking variation. Although not visible in this photo, the nose cap seems to be finished in Yellow. This color indicates that the aircraft was allocated to 3. Staffel in the Gruppe.

The inconsistently applied digits of the werknummer are also of note. "Yellow 5" appears to be finished in a solid upper surface covering of faded RLM 81 Brown-Violet and RLM 82 Light Green.

(left and next page) Three views of an interesting Messerschmitt Me 262A. "White 1" displays the hallmarks of a Kommando Nowotny Stormbird – hard-edged dapple pattern stencil tail, Yellow mid-fuselage band and the individual aircraft number on the forward fuselage. This aircraft also bears a White letter "S" under the tail surfaces. The meaning of this supplementary letter is not certain, but it might indicate an aircraft of the Staff Flight. Other sources propose that it stands for Schule suggesting a training aircraft or an instructional airframe.

Two views of Messerschmitt Me 262A, W. Nr. 110956 "White 17" of EJG 2 photographed at Lechfeld in Germany. This aircraft wears the "White S" marking in the center of the Balkenkreuz and forward of the Hakenkreuz. A Yellow band is painted around the mid-fuselage.

Yet another variation in the style of the "White S" on "White 14" seen at Lechfeld Airbase.

It is interesting to note the use of the mid-war style Black-White-Black Balkenkreuz on the lower wing of this Messerschmitt Me 262, W. Nr. 111891. The photograph was taken at Kitzingen, Germany during April 1945. Messerschmitt Bf 110G-4s lie in the background wearing their final color scheme of solid RLM 75 Gray-Violet over RLM 76 Light Blue.

This is Messerschmitt Me 262 "Yellow 3" photographed on a scrapheap at München-Riem in Germany during late 1945 or 1946. Looks like a skull and crossbones emblem under cockpit. This Stormbird was attached to III./KG(J) 54.

The badge under the cockpit is the **Totenkopf** (Death's Head) emblem of the unit painted on a Yellow shield. The Yellow shield indicated the third **Staffel** of the **Gruppe** – 9./KG(J) 54.

An overpainted diagonal band is clearly visible in this picture. This was possibly a Yellow band to identify a III. **Gruppe** aircraft, or it may be a relic of earlier service. Paint is applied thinly. Putty lines may be seen below the camouflage finish.

Messerschmitt Me 262A-1a of I./JG 7, W.Nr. 112385, "Yellow 8". This 3. Staffel aircraft carries the Red/Blue RV bands and the "running greyhound" badge of JG 7.

An Me 262 A-1a Jabo of III./KG(J) 54 with the wavy White overpainted lines. The White nose cap represents the color of the 7. Staffel, (White) and the Yellow band behind the Black trim represents the color of the III. Gruppe, (Yellow). March 1945, Neuberg near Frankfurt, Germany

Messerschmitt Me 262A-2a, W. Nr. 500200 "Black X"

Introduction: "Black X" enters the scene

Only one Messerschmitt Me 262 of the bomber variant survives today.

"Black X", *Werknummer* 500200 (9K+XK), was built outdoors sometime around February 1945, probably at the Regensburg Waldwerk at Obertraubling.

There was also a flight testing facility at this location. The jet served with a bomber unit, 2 *Staffel* KG 51, for the remainder of the war before being surrendered by its pilot to the RAF.

Test flown by the Royal Aircraft Establishment, it was subsequently sent out to Australia as a mark of gratitude from the British people. It remains in the collection of the Australian War Memorial.

The pilot of "Black X" was *Fahenjunker-Oberfeldwebel* Hans-Robert Fröhlich.

Fröhlich was born 5 March 1914. He was posted to I./KG 51 in Berlin at the beginning of 1945, just in time to see out the war flying "Black X".

After the war he served with the *Kriminalpolizei* in Hamburg before retiring in 1972.

Hans-Robert Fröhlich seemed to put his war behind him and, presumably with the exception of his KG 51 comrades, did not speak of it.

Although his aircraft survives, Fröhlich himself remains widely known only as the pilot of one of the last surviving jets of the Second World War.

KG 51: The "Crop Damage" *Geschwader*

The decision to initially produce the Messerschmitt Me 262 as a bomber, rather than as a pure fighter, and the role this decision played in the type's introduction to service is well known and needs no further discussion here. Suffice it to say that the chronicler of *Kampfgeschwader* 51 proudly recorded that, as in the past, the 'Edelweiss' *Geschwader* had the honor of introducing yet another new type into combat.

Some pilots of KG 51 were introduced to the Me 262 on 20 June 1944, a fortnight after the Allied landings in Normandy. KG 51 seems to have been relatively generously equipped with the jet type, if only briefly: 60 aircraft from the Trials Detachment of KG 51 were recorded in early June as lost to a USAAF raid on Lechfeld.

A month later, the pilots of 3. *Staffel* had accumulated about four flights each with the new type, and were therefore considered ready for operations. Missions commenced out of Châteaudun, using nine aircraft, after 20 July 1944. The newly operational 3. *Staffel* was detached as *Kommando Schenk*, after its commanding officer. Shortly thereafter, on 12 August, the unit had to move on to Ètampes as a result of Allied pressure, and then to Juvincourt on 22 August, where the *Kommando* was reinforced by 3./KG 51 a day later. It is symptomatic of Me 262 operations that only five of the nine aircraft sent as the reinforcements arrived. Two crashed on take-off from Lechfeld, another crashed on take-off from the intermediate stop at Schwabisch-Hall, while the pilot of the fourth aircraft became lost, could not find Juvincourt and made a forced landing.

Major Wolfgang Schenk was a very experienced pilot, with a varied combat career. Having joined the *Luftwaffe* in 1936, he served first with I./JG "Richthofen" and then I./ZG 1 for the campaigns in Poland, Norway and France. On 16 May 1940, Schenk was shot down and badly injured by a RAF Hurricane. It was not until September 1940 that he was sufficiently recovered to fly again. He was made *Staffelkapitän* of 1./ *Erprobungsgruppe 210*, which became 1./SKG 210 in April 1941 and took part in the invasion of Russia. After leading *Erprobungsstaffel 210*, by 1 January 1942 Schenk was *Kommandeur* of I./ZG 1. A year later Schenk took over Sch.G. 2 and flew ground-attack Fw 190 fighters on the Mediterranean front. Schenk was injured again in December 1943 and was moved to a position as an inspector at the *Reisestab*. In March 1944 he was appointed as a technical advisor at the *Luftwaffe*'s technical department and became responsible for bombing trials with the Me 262 in June. Schenk was well qualified to undertake this difficult task. Aside from his leadership abilities, he was a very capable dual-engine pilot, had suffered all the joys and tribulations of introducing a new and troubled aircraft into frontline units (the Me 210) and he had combat experience using a high-performance fighter in the ground-attack role.

Despite being ostensibly a fully fledged bomber, the Me 262 lacked a specialized bomb sight. It was also forbidden for security reasons to make diving attacks, or operate below 4,000 meters, both of which were considered to make the aircraft more vulnerable to ground fire and thus make it more likely for a specimen to fall into Allied hands. The frustrating inaccuracy of bombing attacks led to the pilots referring to their unit as the "Crop Damage *Geschwader*". More soberly, Fritz Wendel reported:

In level flight, the Revi was useless for accurate bombing. Pinpoint targets could not be hit. Kommando Schenk *was therefore unable to claim any tactical success.*

Kommando Schenk continued daily operations with a maximum of nine serviceable aircraft until 4 September 1944, when the unit moved across the German frontier and merged with I./KG 51, now sufficiently equipped with Me 262s to begin operations, although the *Kommando* remained in existence until the end of October, when it was formally integrated back into its parent unit. Under Allied pressure, the men of KG 51 continued to lead a nomadic lifestyle, moving from one airfield to another to avoid advancing land forces and fighter-bombers.

On 8 September 1944, the Allies were provided with their first chance to examine a Me 262. It was an aircraft from *Kommando Schenk*, and perhaps fulfilled the fears that had led to the altitude restrictions on jet operations. *Leutnant* Rolf Weidman, flying a Me 262A-1a, W. Nr. 170040 (9K+OL) was shot down by antiaircraft fire near Diest in Belgium. Its engines were recovered and sent to Britain.

Throughout late September and most of October, *Kommando Schenk* continued almost daily operations against Allied ground forces in Belgium and the Netherlands. Some of their missions were coordinated by *Gefechtsverband Hallensleben*, a command that organized night operations by those *Luftwaffe* units operating on the Western Front. I./KG 51 was attached to this command later in 1944, but it is unclear whether the unit's Me 262 jets were used for night missions.

Kommando Schenk flew its last sorties under its own name, weather reconnaissance flights over Maas, on 25 October 1944. The unit's last losses occurred the following day. One aircraft was destroyed and another damaged on the ground at Rhein by an RAF raid. During its existence, the *Kommando* had received 25 Me 262 jets, of which 23 appear to have been lost to all causes, and flown around 400 sorties in the face of bad weather and Allied opponents, in particular the Tempest V fighters of No. 3 Squadron RAF. The *Kommando* lost four pilots killed.

At the same time that *Kommando Schenk* was formally reabsorbed into its parent unit, I./KG 51, debate was continuing over the production of the Me 262. Contrary to Hitler's desires, 52 Me 262 jets had been built as fighters during October 1944 and issued to *Kommondo Nowotny*, the same number as had gone to KG 51. During a conference of 1 to 4 November 1944, Hitler authorized the production the Me 262 as a fighter, on the proviso that it still be capable of carrying two 500kg bombs. Despite this change, the bulk of Me 262s produced during November 1944 went to KG 51. By December, however, this had changed, and all those Me 262s that made it beyond the factory doors that month went to fighter squadrons. II./KG 51

converted to the Me 262 at Schwabisch-Hall in October 1944, joining I./KG 51 at Hopsten until February 1945.

I./KG 51 took part in the infamous Operation *Bodenplatte* on 1 January 1945. The unit's targets were the airfields at Eindhoven and Hertogenbosch. I./KG 51 put up 21 Me 262s for this operation, and these led the way to their targets, undertaking the initial bombing run, which was followed up by strafing piston-engine fighters. This was the largest number of Me 262s ever used by KG 51 for a single operation. One Me 262 was claimed shot down and another damaged by anti-aircraft fire at Gilze-Rijn. Thus far, no evidence has been found to confirm any KG 51 losses on this day. Elsewhere, three Me 262s were lost on 1 January 1945, but these were all from the fighter unit, JG 7, and lost as a result of air combat.

KG 51 was moving from one airfield to another, matching the retreat of the German army. Unlike KG 54, KG 51 remained operating predominantly in the bomber role up until the cessation of hostilities, rather than switching to a solely fighter role. Nonetheless, some pilots of KG 51 were successful in air combat. *Leutnant* Wilhelm Batel, of 2. *Staffel*, shot down an USAAF P-47 in March 1945, almost certainly after dispensing with his external ordnance.

The carriage of bombs reduced the top speed of the Me 262 to such a degree that late-model Spitfires could catch it. *Feldwebel* Rudolf Hoffmann, for example, of I./KG 51, flying Me 262A-2a *werknummer* 110615 (possibly 9K+NL), was shot down on 14 February 1945 by Flight Lieutenant Tony Gaze, the only Australian pilot to shoot down a Me 262. Flying a Spitfire XIV with 601 Squadron, Gaze caught the Me 262, one of three, in a straight-line pursuit. Gaze fired on the starboard-most aircraft of a *Kette* of three bombers, setting its starboard engine alight. The jet dived into the clouds and Gaze's wingman reported it crashing near Emmerick. The unsuspecting Hoffmann had perhaps thought he still had the edge in speed, despite carrying two bombs. He was not cautious enough.

Messerschmitt Me 262A-1a, W. Nr. 110836, "Black L". This Stormbird was also attached to I./KG 51. Note the thinly outlined Black identification letter and the Red capped tail indicating an aircraft of 2. Staffel. The Red cap appears to have a very thin White outline on its lower border. The crude overpainting of an earlier identification seems to suggest that "Black L" was hastily reassigned!

On 30 March 1945, IV./KG 51 bowed to the inevitable and surrendered its aircraft, and some of its pilots, to JV 44 to serve as fighters. Throughout April 1945, however, there was much confusion over who actually controlled the jet aircraft of KG 51. In early April, KG 51 had been assigned to IX.(*J*) *Fliegerkorps*, but by mid-April was reassigned to *Luftwaffenkommando West*. At the same time, IX. (*J*) *Fliegerkorps* ordered KG(J) 55 disbanded and its ground equipment and vehicles handed over to II./KG 51. Confused, the latter unit sat tight at Hörsching waiting to see who was actually in charge.

Others took the initiative. Stuka ace *Major* Heinrich Brücker flew his command, I./KG 51, direct to Riem on 23 April 1945 and joined JV 44. It is not known whether Brücker flew any missions with JV 44, but a listing of 26 April indicated that he brought about nine jets with him to the *Jagdverband*. Other first *Gruppe* aircraft seem to have gone elsewhere, although the situation is far from clear.

Hauptmann *Abrahamczik with a Messerschmitt Me 262 of I./KG 51 in early 1945. Note the small, stenciled "9K" on the port fuselage side just forward of the* **Balkenkreuz.**

A list sent to *Luftflottenkommando* 6 to 27 April 1945 shows several KG 51 pilots on strength with JV 44:

Major Brücker	I./KG 51
Leutnant Strate	I./KG 51
Obergefreiter Weindl	I./KG 51
Fahenjunker-Oberfeldwebel Fröhlich	I./KG 51
Feldwebel Trenke	I./KG 51
Unteroffizier Pöhling	II./KG 51

Although Fröhlich appears to have passed through JV 44 in late April before moving on to Czechoslovakia, his aircraft "Black X" is not recorded as on strength with JV 44 at all. it is possible that Fröhlich obtained "Black X" once he volunteered to go to Czechoslovakia and thus required a bomber variant.

For a small number of crews from I and II *Gruppen*, the constant change of airfields ahead of the Allied advance led eventually to Czechoslovakia and Prague. On 30 April 1945, *Hauptmann* Rudolf Abrahamczik led a group of seven volunteers and their aircraft, from I./KG 51, to Prague. *Oberleutnant* Wolfgang Baetz took a similar number of volunteers from II./KG 51 to the same location. This lead to the novel situation of pilots attempting to offer close support to ground forces fighting in an urban environment while flying one of the fastest aircraft of the war.

On 6 May 1945, Prague was evacuated and the remaining Me 262s were flown to Zatec. The ground crew, following by road, never arrived. On 8 May, following the signing of the instrument of German surrender, Abrahamczik instructed his remaining pilots to surrender to either US or British forces.

On the afternoon of 8 May, four Me 262s took off from Zatec and headed west. These were the only 2./KG 51 jet aircraft to survive the war. Abrahamczik and *Leutnant* Häeffner flew to München-Riem and surrendered to US forces. They had been unable to venture further afield because Häeffner's aircraft was unable to retract its undercarriage.

Leutnant Batel, in 9K+FB, and Fröhlich, in 9K+XK ("Black X"), resolved to surrender to the British. Batel, however, was able to navigate his way to his parent's farm near Pommoissel and made a wheels-up landing in nearby field. He walked home.

Fröhlich flew first to Hamburg, but the runway was obstructed and thus too short. He flew on to Fassberg in the Netherlands, an airstrip with which he was apparently familiar, landed and surrendered to the RAF and RCAF units that had occupied the airfield. The RAF personnel were celebrating the end of hostilities and took the *Luftwaffe* officer in for a drink. It was two days before anyone thought to relieve Fröhlich of his pistol and he was sent into internment.

Hptm. Rudolf Abrahamczik from I./KG 51, who led a group of seven voluneeers and their aircraft on ground support duties to Prague.

"Black X" of I./KG 51 at Fassberg in 1945 (Bill Harper via Robert Bracken)

Under RAF Colors

While at Fassberg, "Black X" was selected by the RAF for evaluation. British national markings (excluding the fin flash) were painted over the *Balkenkreuz* and the aircraft was allocated the Air Ministry number 81. "Air Min 81" was painted in White on the port side of the aft fuselage. A Yellow prototype "P" in a ring was also added.

Aside from the national markings, the only other modification made to the aircraft was the removal of the FuG 16ZY radio set (VHF R/T, D/F and retransmission facilities for ground control stations) and its replacement with British equipment. The most obvious result of this was the removal of the external D/F loop aerial. This aerial was not returned to the aircraft before it was shipped to Australia.

Staging via Melsbroek, "Black X" was flown to Manston (in Kent) on 28 August 1945. Its pilot was Squadron Leader A.F. Martindale, commanding officer of the Aerodynamics Flight of the Royal Aircraft Establishment. Once a hydraulic problem was rectified, "Black X" flew on to Farnborough on 6 September 1945, the only time the aircraft was not flown by Martindale.

"Black X" made eleven flights with the Royal Aircraft Establishment, including five flights to publicly display the aircraft, and logged 5 hours, 35 minutes of flight time. On 26 April 1946 "Black X" was allocated the RAF serial VP554 and was destined for further testing. This did not occur.

In August 1946 "Black X" was packed up for shipping to Australia and arrived in Melbourne on 22 December 1946.

Camouflage and Markings of "Black X"

"Black X" at Fassberg, Germany in 1945 (Cecil Mann via Robert Bracken)

"Black X" Today

"Black X" is an important and unique relic of the Second World War

It is the only Messerschmitt Me 262 bomber variant to survive today. "Black X" is also the only remaining Me 262 to retain its original paint.

Although "Black X" is undoubtedly scruffy and suffering from at least three rounds of repainting, it is still a good representation of the Messerschmitt Me 262 in service; especially when compared to the "as-new" restorations of the type elsewhere in the world.

The aircraft may eventually be reassembled when space permits, but the historical value of its finish will ensure that it is not repainted in the foreseeable future.

"Black X" Genesis

Messerschmitt Me 262A-2a, *Werknummer* 500200, was built by Messerschmitt AG at Regensburg as the last of the 500101-500200 construction block. The aircraft was most likely completed and test flown in February 1945.

The majority of the aircraft shell is constructed from 'Alclad' alloy panels. However, the aircraft nose, engine nacelles and a panel on the underside of the fuselage are steel. Furthermore, wood panels are used on the leading edge of the tail surfaces and the undercarriage doors.

German fighters at this late stage of the war were rushed into service with little regard to production quality or camouflage standardization. "Black X" displays a great deal of evidence pointing to its hasty manufacture. For example, the aft fuselage is misaligned with no apparent attempt at correction prior to service entry.

"Black X" in Australia

"Black X" arrived in Australia on 22 December 1946.

The Royal Australian Air Force was given little notice of the impending arrival of this war prize. Without proper display or restoration facilities, "Black X" was therefore placed in storage at Laverton RAAF base where it remained in crates until 1948. Thereafter it was transferred to the Australian War Memorial's warehouse in Sydney.

When the decision was taken to display the aircraft some seven years later, "Black X" was sent to the RAAF for repainting. Australian War Memorial staff offered no advice on how the aircraft should appear, so the aircraft was painted in RAAF Foliage Green (upper surfaces) and light Blue (lower surfaces). *Balkenkreuz* and *Hakenkreuz* were applied, but the Red fin tip and nose cap were left untouched.

"Black X" was displayed in this condition in the Aeroplane Hall of the Australian War Memorial between 1955 and 1970.

"Black X" was loaned to the RAAF Museum at Point Cook after coming off display. The aircraft's undercarriage collapsed during transfer, crushing the lateral nosewheel door. Superficial damage to the fuselage was repaired.

The hanger conditions at bayside Point Cook were not favorable to the long-term preservation of the aircraft. Its surface condition deteriorated noticeably during this period.

Paint Archaeology;
Examining the layered finishes
of "Black X"

By 1980, there was some confusion about the actual identity of the Australian War Memorial's Messerschmitt Me 262. At this stage most of its original markings, including the *werknummer*, were hidden by the RAAF's spurious repainting.

It was therefore decided to retrieve the aircraft from Point Cook and, with RAAF cooperation, to remove the 1955 paint.

Noted aviation historian Ken Merrick joined a team from the Australian War Memorial and the RAAF to uncover the original colors and markings, and to answer the following questions:

Was the aircraft *werknummer* 500210 or 500200? Did the aircraft have the wing from *werknummer* 112372 (Air Min 51 – often confused with Air Min 81 in photographs)? Was the entire aircraft *werknummer* 112372?

Removal of the 1955 paint successfully resolved these issues. The aircraft was proven to be W. Nr. 500200 (as British records had indicated all along) and it retained its original wing.

The service history of the aircraft was confirmed by the resurrected markings. The "Red X" that was thought to have been seen through peeling paint in the 1950s turned out to be a "Black X", supplying the clue that was needed to trace the aircraft's history. Furthermore, examination of the starboard nose revealed the number "200", confirming the aircraft's identity as *werknummer* 500200. Traces of the *werknummer* were also uncovered on the port side of the tail.

The identity of the wing was resolved by examining the original painted finish. Camouflage mapping matched the colors of the wing and the upper fuselage. This suggested that "Black X" retained its original wing.

Following removal of the 1955 paint, the aircraft was moved to Canberra and went into storage at the Memorial's Mitchell Annex. In 1994 it was moved to the Treloar Technology Centre.

As of the end of 2001, "Black X" remains in storage in a disassembled state.

Parts Manual Diagrams

Fuselage front section

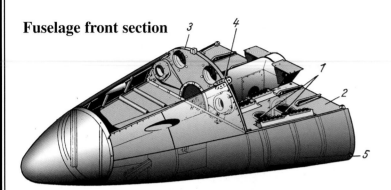

1. Ammo boxes
2. Bulkhead
3. Weapon frame
4. Support strut attachment
5. Lower attachment

Cockpit

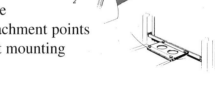

1. Tube
2. Attachment points
3. Seat mounting
4. Pot

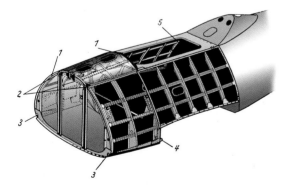

Fuselage Center section

1. Bulkhead
2. Support struts for attachment of fuselage front section
3. Lower attachment of fuselage front section
4. Wing junction front
5. Assembly opening for cockpit tube

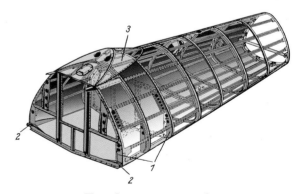

Fuselage rear section

1. Bulkhead
2. Wing junction rear
3. Fairing aid for aerodynamic foil

Parts Manual Diagrams

Vertical Tail

1. Vertical Tail
2. Cap

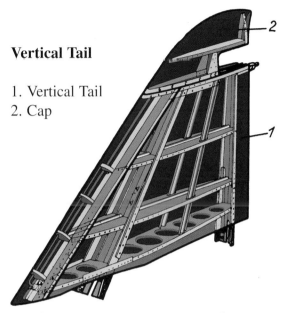

Rudder

1. Rudder
2. Cap
3. End Cap

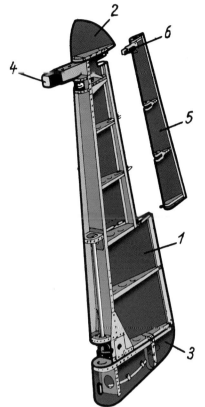

Tail Unit Mounting

1. Attachment frame for horizontal tail
2. Oblique frame, front attachment for vertical tail
3. Oblique frame, rear attachment for vertical tail
4. Bearing for horizontal tail

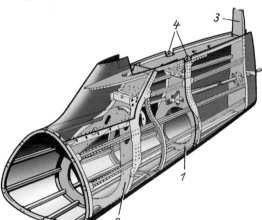

Left Wing (right wing mirror image of left wing)

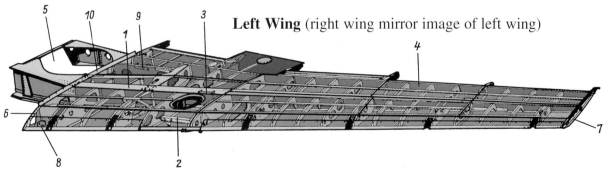

1. Main spar
2. Front engine mounting attachment
3. Rear engine mounting
4. Auxiliary spar

5. Undercart housing
6. Rib 1
7. Rib 21
8. Front point of attachment

9. Rear point of attachment
10. Shaped profile

Luftwaffe Colors Observed on "Black X"		
RLM Color	**Federal Standard Equivalent**	**Usage**
RLM 02 Gray	Slightly darker than FS 34424	This color is noticeably lighter than than samples of RLM 02 found in other reliable sources including Eagle Editions' *Luftwaffe Color Chart* and *The Official Monogram Guide to Painting German Aircraft 1935-1945* (see References). It is applied as an undercoat for some steel surfaces and for control surfaces.
RLM 23 Red	Slightly Brighter and less Orange than FS 21310	This color is in excellent condition as it has escaped post-war repainting. It is a close match for the RLM 23 *Rot* sample in Eagle Editions' *Luftwaffe Color Chart*; and somewhat brighter than the sample in *The Official Monogram Guide to Painting German Aircraft 1935-1945*.
RLM 76 Light Blue	Slightly darker than FS 34670	The bulk of the lower nose is painted in this color. It is slightly lighter and slightly Greener than samples of RLM 76 found in other reliable sources.
RLM 76 Light Blue (variation)	Good match for FS 35622	Applied to the bomb racks. This color is paler than samples of RLM 76 found in other reliable sources. It is a fair match for the color labeled Gray-Blue in *The Official Monogram Guide to Painting German Aircraft 1935-1945*.
RLM 81 Brown-Violet	Slightly lighter than FS 33070	Good match for a faded version of the RLM 81 sample in Eagle Editions' *Luftwaffe Color Chart*.
RLM 82 Light Green	Similar to FS 34258 but less Olive	Due to its thin application over bare metal, this color probably appears much lighter than in its undiluted version. The actual shade varied widely on the airframe depending on the surface preparation and condition.
Cream Yellow Primer	No close equivalent	Slightly darker than the RLM 05 sample on page 139 of *The Official Monogram Guide to Painting German Aircraft 1935-1945*.
Red Primer	Darker than FS 31310	Red Color with an Orange tint.
Dark Gray Primer / Filler	Possibly similar to FS 36081	Dark, Neutral Gray. Very little of the color is directly visible on the surface of the airframe.

Table: Summary of Color Observations

"Black X"
General Paint Features

Exterior
Primer and Undercoat

The wings and the majority of the fuselage of "Black X" were constructed of an alloy that did not require further preparation before camouflage painting.

Undercoat or primer was therefore only applied to the non-alloy elements of the airframe. These included the steel fuselage nose and engine nacelles; plus wooden components such as the undercarriage doors and leading edge of the fin.

The nose displays evidence of at least two undercoat colors. One color closely matches RLM 02 Gray (with a Federal Standard equivalent a little darker than FS 34424) and a Cream color similar to RLM 05.

The wooden fillet on the leading edge of the fin appears to be sealed with pinked fabric. Patches of this fabric and its sawtooth demarcation can be clearly seen underneath chipped paint on the tail surfaces.

The fabric is finished in Red primer under the camouflage finish. Red primer is also revealed under the camouflage paint on the leading edges of the horizontal tail surfaces.

Control surfaces have been undercoated with RLM 02. The lower surfaces of the ailerons retained this color in Luftwaffe service. Putty has been extensively applied to panel lines. The majority of the putty is hidden beneath the original German camouflage and the Australian paint.

Glimpses of the putty on the lower wing suggest that it is a Dark Gray color possibly matching FS 36081.

Upper Fuselage

The original medium Green color can be clearly seen adjacent to the fuselage cross. This color is more than likely RLM 82. The darker surrounding Green is RAAF Foliage Green. The upper surface camouflage seems to follow the 20 February 1945 RLM directive for the application of RLM 81 **Braunviolet** and RLM 82 **Hellgrün** to the Messerschmitt Me 262.

However, upper surface camouflage is thinly applied, making it difficult to classify the colors with certainty. This difficulty is compounded by the wide variation in shade and hue demonstrated by late-war **Luftwaffe** colors.

A dirty Olive-Brown color can be identified on patches of the fuselage and inside the port side **Balkenkreuz**. The color is slightly lighter than Federal Standard paint color FS 33070. This is consistent with the range of shades officially labeled RLM 81 Brown-Violet.

The bulk of the upper fuselage is finished in a medium Green color similar to FS 34258, but less Olive. Although this color is not as bright as some other samples, it is still

likely to be RLM 82 Light Green. Due to its thin application over bare metal, this color probably appears much lighter than in its undiluted version. The actual shade varies widely on the airframe depending on the surface preparation and condition. Both of these colors were hastily applied over bare metal, showing runs and resulting in a translucent finish.

Putty lines and undercoat (on the nose) are very obvious across the entire airframe. The camouflage on the nose is also notable for its streaky horizontal application.

The Green color has been applied to the fin and rudder in a dense, cloudy finish. Patches of a pale color (most likely RLM 76 Light Blue) can be seen through the Green paint, especially toward the top of the fin and the rudder. An infrequent mottle of RLM 81 Brown-Violet appears in spots on the fin, rudder and empennage.

The colors have otherwise been applied in a standard pattern. This further points to "Black X"s' completion date as some time after February 1945.

Lower Fuselage

The original finish of the lower rear fuselage was oxide-coated, unpainted alloy. The appearance would have been that of flat-finished metal. The Australian-applied Light Blue on the lower rear fuselage is flaking off due to a layer of grease on the metal under the overpainting. It is interesting to note that the color of the Australian Blue paint is equivalent to FS35622 – a good match for the Luftwaffe color RLM 76 Light Blue

The lower nose of "Black X" is finished in a Light Blue that is slightly darker than FS34670. This color is almost certainly a variation of RLM 76 Light Blue. The bomb racks are painted in a paler version of RLM 76. They are a good match for FS35622.

Some patches of primer are evident on the nose around the camouflage demarcation line on the fuselage side.

This primer is probably RLM 02 Gray. This color is slightly darker than FS34424.

Cream-colored primer is also visible under damaged paintwork on the underside of the nose. This color is somewhat similar to samples of RLM 05 Cream Yellow.

Upper Wings

Contrast between colors on the upper wings is very low. In fact, it is difficult to discern any camouflage pattern on the wings in the aircraft's present condition. However, patches of color are visible. These match the RLM 81 Brown-Violet and RLM 82 Light Green colors that also appear on the upper fuselage. It is reasonable to assume that the camouflage on the upper wings was applied according to a standard pattern.

Lower Wings

The lower wings were unpainted when the aircraft was captured. The pale Blue paint currently on the lower wings was applied by the Royal Australian Air Force during their 1955 refurbishment.

Fortunately, stencilling on the lower wing was masked during the painting process. These original German stencils were applied in Black.

Some of these masked-off sections also display fragments of the dark Gray putty used to seal gaps between panels. The putty was applied directly to the bare metal, and stencil data was sprayed over the top of the putty.

Very little of the putty is directly visible on the surface of the airframe. However, it appears to be a very dark neutral Gray, possibly similar to FS 36081.

The engine nacelles have been removed from the wings revealing large areas of bare metal on the lower wing. (See photo next page.)

Faint stamped markings can be observed on the bare metal. These stamps were probably applied to the sheet metal prior to construction of the airframe.

Lower Wings

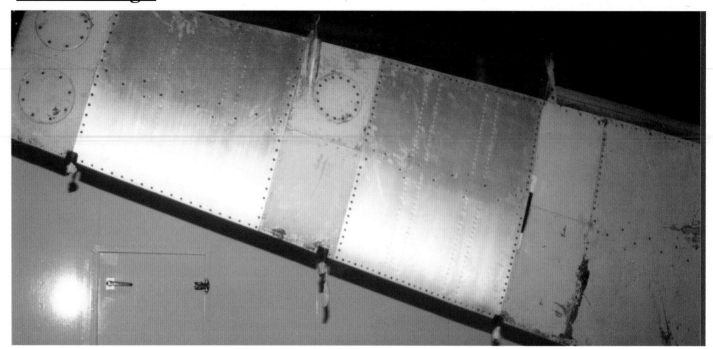

Engine Nacelles

The nacelles were originally finished in RLM 76 with the entire rear section painted Black. The camouflage on the forward upper area of the nacelles was consistent with the scheme on the upper wings.

The Jumo 004 power plants still wear a translucent Red coat of preservative that was probably applied before "Black X"'s sea journey to Australia. As displayed today, the engine nacelles are finished in the Australian colors applied in 1955.

Undercarriage

Gear legs are finished in RLM 02 Gray. The wheel hubs were probably originally finished in semi-gloss Black, but the main wheels currently have the appearance of oxidized alloy.

The undercarriage doors are fabricated from wood. These are painted in a pale Blue color that is a fair match for RLM 76.

Interior

The cannon bay and airframe interior remain in excellent original condition.

The interior of the cannon bay is largely unpainted, although the inside of the clamshell doors and framing reinforcement are finished in RLM 02 Gray.

The four 30mm MK108 cannon are unpainted gunmetal.

The main gear bay is not blocked off from the central fuselage interior. The fuselage interior and the exterior of the cockpit tub are also unpainted alloy.

Interior (Continued)

The fuselage interior and the exterior of the cockpit tub.

Forward Fuselage

The port side lower nose. This area is painted RLM 76 Light Blue. Red primer is evident around the shell ejector ports where tape has removed the camouflage paint.

The interior of the cannon access hatch. This is original RLM 02 Gray in almost perfect condition. The prop to keep the hatch open can be seen in the upper right-hand corner of the image.

Markings

*The fuselage **Balkenkreuz** is the White outline style. It is particularly interesting to note that both the fuselage **Balkenkreuz** are tilted slightly forward when referenced against vertical panel lines.*

*The tail **Hakenkreuz** was plain Black in service, but restoration of the original factory paintwork suggests that it may have worn a thin White outline at some stage. Upper wing crosses are a White outline, and the lower wing crosses are Black and White. British roundels and the Australian "German" markings are still visible on the airframe.*

*The Black **werknummer** is stencilled just above the horizontal tail surfaces. The fin tip and nose cap are RLM 23 Red.*

*The "Black X" marking, derived from the aircraft's **Verbandskennzeichen** (9K + XK), was Black with a thin White outline. The last three digits of the **werknummer**, 200, are present in Black on either side of the nose. A very thin, faint Red outline seems to surround the numbers on the starboard side. The zeros seem to have been applied with a stencil, but the style and width of the '2' on the port side is quite different to the same digit on the starboard side.*

Some additional data has been hand-painted on the fuselage. Much of this data was clearly applied by British or Australian authorities but some, including a small Red "100" seen forward of the "200" nose marking, may be original.

(above and below) The cannon bay is in excellent original condition. All four 30mm MK108 are fitted. The cannon and the bay itself remain unpainted. Note the German factory stencilling on the rear bulkhead. The steel reinforcement strut is painted RLM 02 Gray. The top of this part has corroded where the paint has worn away. The Gray electrical boxes and Yellow cables are in remarkable order.

(above and below) The port side of the nose displays a streaky application of the darker color over a very thin coat of RLM 82 Light Green. Very large sections of RLM 02 Gray primer are visible on the cannon access hatch.

The number "200" is hand-painted in Black on both sides of the nose. Although the "00" is applied in a stencil style, brush streaks are clearly apparent. This number represents the "last three" digits of the aircraft werknummer – probably an aid to final assembly of this Stormbird's components.

It appears that these numbers were at least partially over-painted by camouflage paint while the aircraft was in service. A number of small markings have been applied by Allied forces. Note the "TRESTLE" just below the "2". The Red border around the cannon ports is the result of covers applied by British forces during evaluation. The Red nose cap is original.

The starboard side of the nose reveals a different style used for the digit "2". The stencilled "00" is clearer in this view. This photograph suggests that the "Black 200" is outlined thinly in Red. The origin and meaning of the small "Red 100" is not known at this time.

The original Red nose cap showing evidence of local repairs after an accident during transport in Australia. The centre of the nose cap has been plugged. This is the position for the clear cover of the BSK 16 Gun Camera.

(above and below) The lower forward fuselage, from the front looking back. The front undercarriage door is missing and the nosewheel can be seen in the forward undercarriage bay. The bomb racks are also prominent in this view.

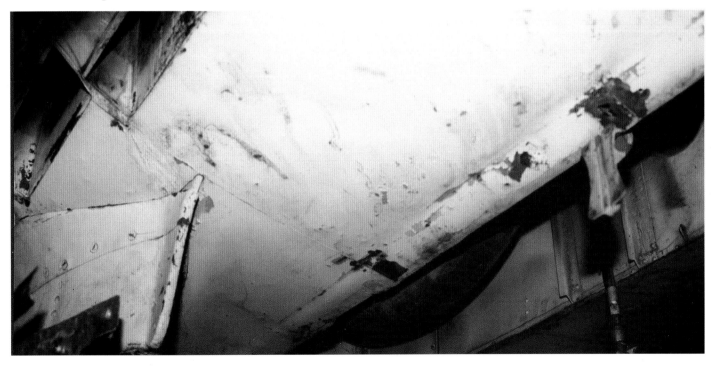

The lower surface of the nose was painted RLM 76 Light Blue. The color on the exterior of the nose is the same as the nose gear bay, so it seems most likely that this is an original German paint application although some evidence of overpainting is present. Patches of Cream Yellow colored primer are showing through flaking paint.

A close-up view of the nose gear bay, from the front looking back. Neither of the doors are fitted, but the bracket for the top door can be seen in the center of the photograph. The top nose gear door was mounted to this bracket via three screws.

The top nose gear door is held separately. This wooden component is finished in RLM 65 Light Blue. Plywood can be seen at the edges of the door, and beneath minor damage.

The three offset holes match the mounting bracket in the photograph above.

It appears that a section of the door was repainted in RAAF Sky Blue, but it is known that "Black X" was present on this part during wartime service. What is not certain is whether both "X"s were on the door at the same time. If so, the top "X" would have been hidden when the undercarriage door was open!

Mid and Rear Fuselage

*The White outline **Balkenkreuz** over the radio access hatch is the original German marking on the starboard side of the mid-fuselage. The Black and White cross aft of the hatch was applied by the RAAF in 1955.*

It is particularly interesting to note that the original fuselage crosses are offset from the vertical. Normally, **Balkenkreuz** on Me 262s are aligned with vertical panel joins. However, this photograph clearly shows that the cross on "Black X" has been applied at an angle. It is, in effect, tilted slightly forward.

*The thin White outline to "Black X" and the base color of RLM 82 Light Green are of note. The offset **Balkenkreuz** is also apparent on this photo of the port side of the fuselage. Patches of RLM 81 Brown-Violet are also plain.*

The crude workmanship applied to late-war **Luftwaffe** *aircraft is strikingly evident in the misaligned panels toward the rear of "Black X".*

Also note the original German stencil markings towards the bottom of the fuselage, just forward of the panel join. These markings were masked over when the aircraft was repainted in 1955.

This rectangle provides an authentic sample of RLM 82 Light Green (on a small section at the left of the masked-off section) and RLM 81 Brown-Violet.

An excellent example of the thin application of RLM 82 Light Green over bare alloy, and its contrasting impact over dark Gray primer/putty.

Dark Gray primer/putty was used extensively on the fuselage to smooth panel joins.

Despite the scruffy appearance of the fuselage, patches of the original colors are still identifiable.

Starboard fuselage side. Note that the fuselage wing root join is unpainted.

Tail Surfaces

The rudder was primed and painted with a thin application of RLM 82 Light Green with patches of RLM 81 Brown-Violet. The vibrant Red tip to the fin and the rudder are original.

The fin has been extensively repainted, but the some of the original Hakenkreuz can be made out. Interestingly, the faint Hakenkreuz below the Australian replica appears to have a White outline although wartime photo-graphs strongly suggest a solid Black swastika was worn while "Black X" was in service. It is possible that the original White outline was overpainted at unit level as an additional camouflage measure.

The fin fairing and empennage. Paint application is consistent with the other alloy components of the fuselage.

Two views of the horizontal stabilizers of "Black X". Although it is impossible to make out a camouflage pattern on these components, they are nevertheless interesting due to the Red-primed strip on the leading edges of the port and starboard stabilizers. Even under the original paintwork, these primed areas would have been identifiable as darker strips of camouflage.

Cockpit Tub / Main Undercarriage Bay

The main undercarriage of the Me 262 retracted into the mid-fuselage interior directly below the cockpit tub. There was no "wheel well" between the gear and the interior of the fuselage.

In accordance with common practice of the late-war period, the fuselage interior was largely unpainted. Strips have simply been primed with RLM 02 Gray along rivet lines and joints.

The fuselage interior is in beautiful condition. Original German stencils and hand-written markings can be seen in this series of photographs.

The photo above is a view from the lower port side, looking forward. The large cylindrical object is the outside of the cockpit tub.

Starboard fuselage interior sidewall. The tubular structural detail is of note.

Wings

Port wing (above) and starboard wing (below).
It is virtually impossible to discern any camouflage pattern on the upper wings in their present condition.

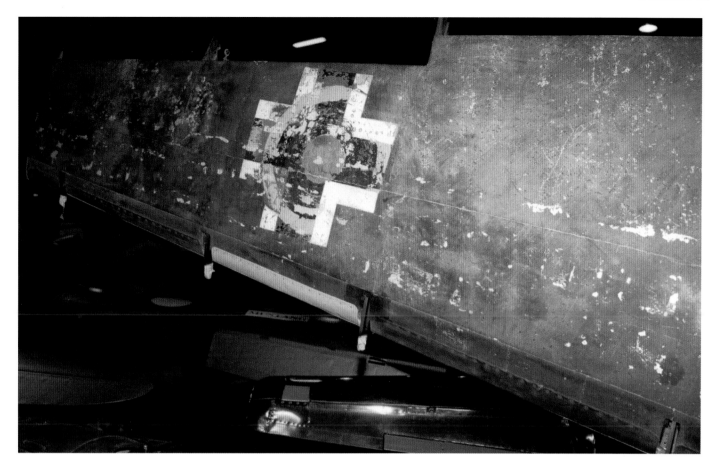

British, Australian and German markings are evident on the upper wings.

Original German stencils were masked over when "Black X" was repainted in 1955. Prior to the Australian refinishing, the entire lower wing was unpainted alloy.

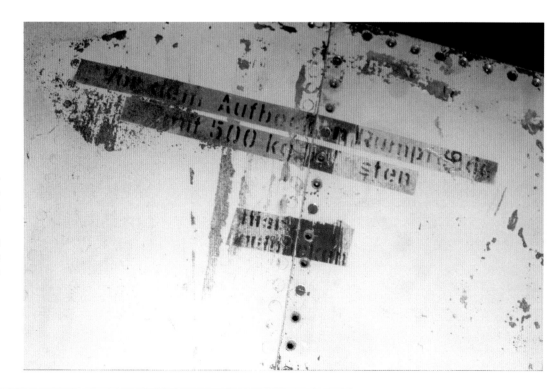

The 1955 repainting did not extend below the engine nacelles. Note the discolored alloy. This was an effect of the extreme heat generated by the Jumo 004 jet engine. Faint signs of factory stamps can be seen on the alloy surface.

Engine

The engine nacelles remain in their Australian colors from 1955. The Red coloration of the Jumo 004 is probably a preservative applied before "Black X's" sea journey in 1948.

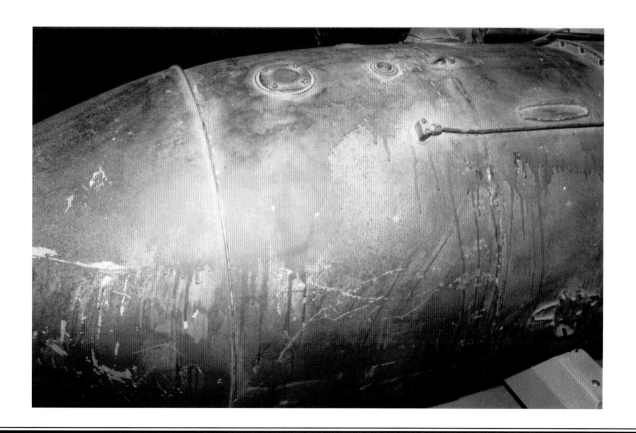

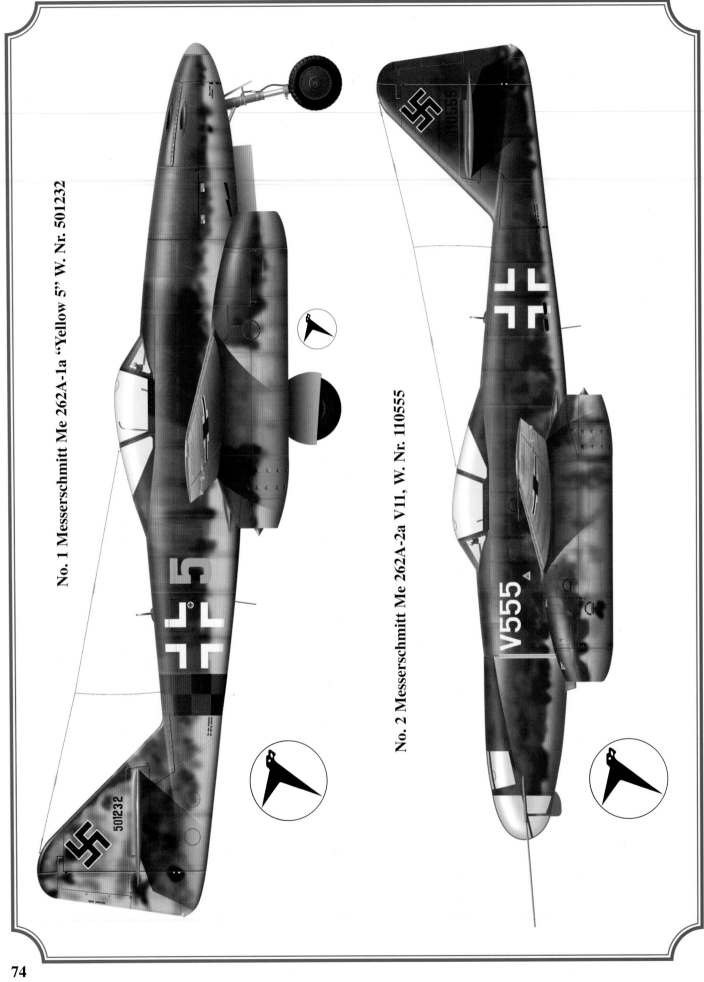

No. 1 Messerschmitt Me 262A-1a "Yellow 5" W. Nr. 501232

No. 2 Messerschmitt Me 262A-2a V11, W. Nr. 110555

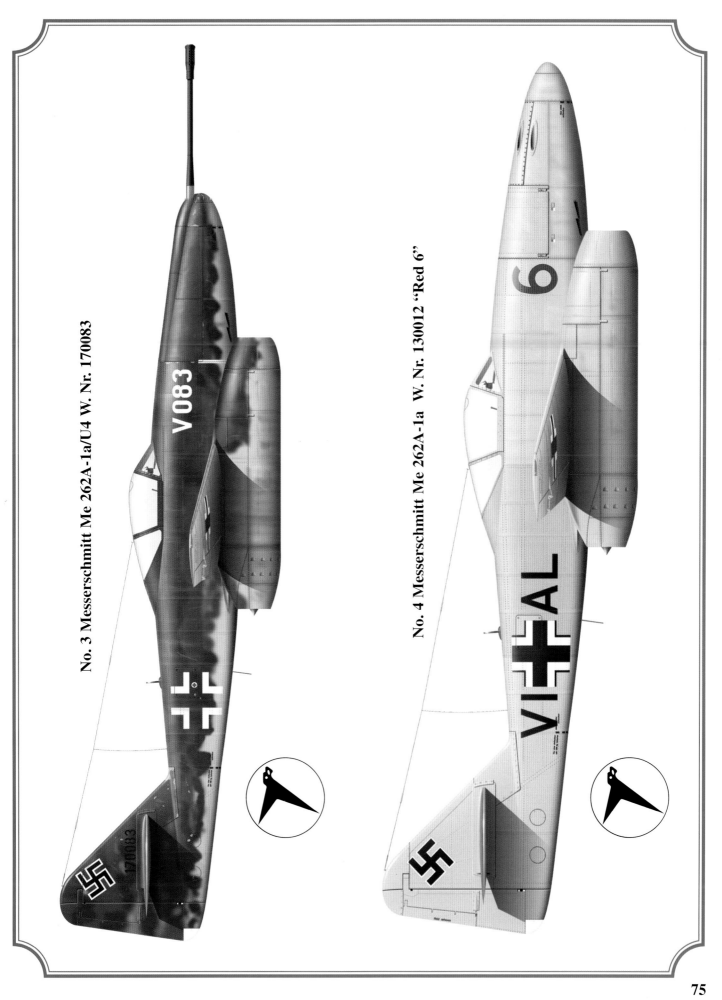

No. 3 Messerschmitt Me 262A-1a/U4 W. Nr. 170083

No. 4 Messerschmitt Me 262A-1a W. Nr. 130012 "Red 6"

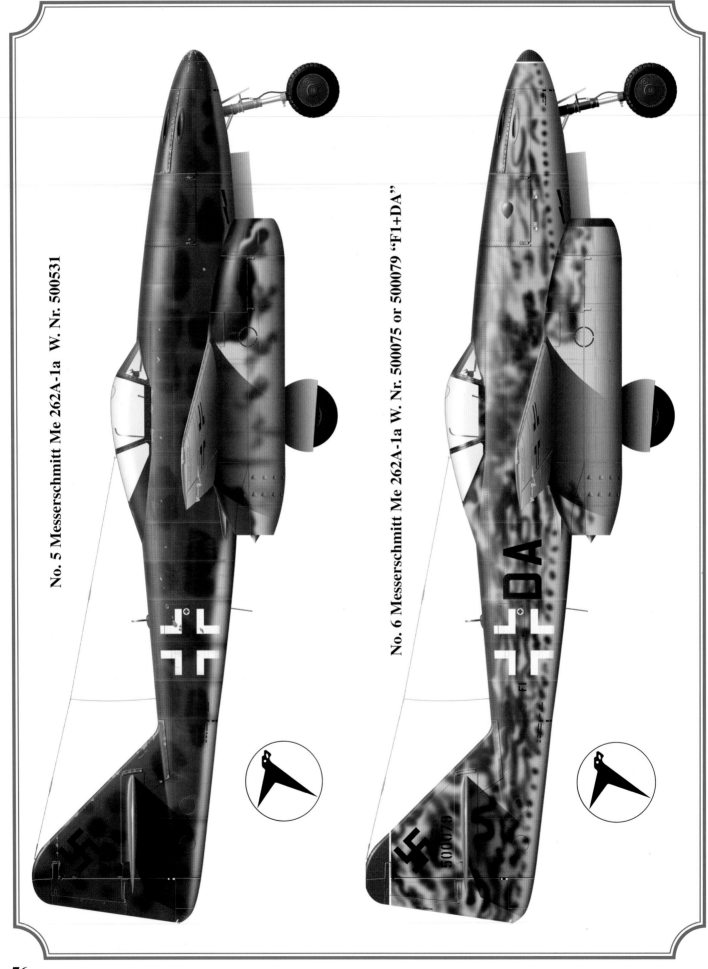

No. 5 Messerschmitt Me 262A-1a W. Nr. 500531

No. 6 Messerschmitt Me 262A-1a W. Nr. 500075 or 500079 "F1+DA"

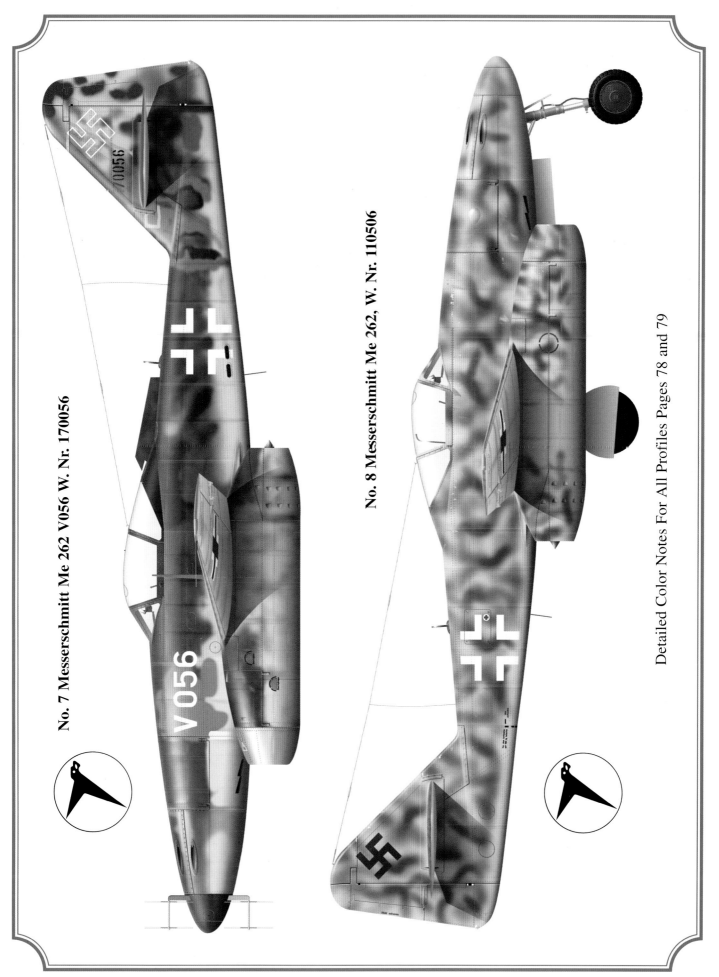

No. 7 Messerschmitt Me 262 V056 W. Nr. 170056

No. 8 Messerschmitt Me 262, W. Nr. 110506

Detailed Color Notes For All Profiles Pages 78 and 79

Profile Color Notes

No. 1 Messerschmitt Me 262A-1a "Yellow 5" W. Nr. 501232

Messerschmitt Me 262A-1a, *werknummer* 501232 "Yellow 5" at München-Riem airfield in Germany during 1945. This aircraft was formerly attached to I./KG (J) 54.

The Red and Black checkered tail band is a particularly interesting marking variation.

The Yellow nose cap indicates that the aircraft was allocated to 3. *Staffel* in the *Gruppe*. The unevenly applied digits of the *werknummer* are also of note.

"Yellow 5" appears to be finished in a solid upper surface covering of faded RLM 81 Brown-Violet and RLM 82 Bright Green.

No. 2 Messerschmitt Me 262A-2a V11, W. Nr. 110555

Messerschmitt Me 262 V11, *werknummer* 110555, was converted in February 1945 as the second prototype Me 262A-2a Fast Bomber with the *Lotfe* gunsight. This variant was intended to vastly improve the bombing accuracy of the Stormbird. The unarmed Me 262 V11 featured a clear nose. As a dedicated bomber variant, it is possible that this aircraft was finished in RLM 70 Black-Green and RLM 71 Dark Green with lower surfaces in RLM 65 Bright Blue.

No. 3 Messerschmitt Me 262A-1a/U4 W. Nr. 170083

Messerschmitt Me 262A-1a/U4 W. Nr. 170083 at Lechfeld Germany during May 1945 was possibly finished in RLM 70 Black-Green and RLM 71 Dark Green upper surfaces. If this was the case, lower surfaces would have been painted RLM 65 Bright Blue. This variant is fitted with a 50 mm cannon.

No. 4 Messerschmitt Me 262A-1a W. Nr. 130012 "Red 6"

Messerschmitt Me 262 S7, V1 + AL. *werknummer* 130012 "Red 6" of *Erprobungskommando* Thierfelder in April or May 1944. This aircraft was finished in overall RLM 76 Light Blue. Radio codes appeared on the fuselage sides and wing undersurfaces in Black. The individual aircraft numbers were carried on the nose in Red. The style of the single digit "6" is quite unusual.

No. 5 Messerschmitt Me 262A-1a W. Nr. 500531

Messerschmitt Me 262A, *werknummer* 500531, at Linz, Austria during 1945. The "chessboard" mottle is of particular interest. The leading edge of the starboard wing displayed a scalloped demarcation. The solid base color is probably RLM 82 Bright Green, while the mottle is either RLM 81 Brown-Violet or RLM 83 Dark Green. The unusual pattern on the starboard engine nacelle is probably the result of a small fire. The opposite side of the rudder features a crudely painted "X" marking. This is most likely an inspection mark applied after capture.

No. 6 Messerschmitt Me 262A-1a W. Nr. 500075 or 500079 "F1+DA"

Messerschmitt Me 262A-1a *werknummer* 500075 or 500079, "F1+DA" at Giebelstadt, Germany in April 1945.

This fascinating Stormbird is finished in a low contrast, squiggly application of RLM 81 Brown-Violet and RLM 83 Dark Green over RLM 76 lower surfaces. The line of spots dividing the colors of the upper and lower fuselage is of particular interest.

The nose cap and fin tip are painted Red, separated from the camouflage finish by a narrow White line. The rim of the jet intakes are also painted Red.

The nose gear door is marked with the letter "D" followed by a tiny letter "A". Both letters appear to be painted in Black. Also note that the forward gear strut appears to be very dark. The color looks more like RLM 66 Black Gray than the specified RLM 02 Gray.

According to the standard *Luftwaffe* bomber identification scheme, "F1" indicates KG 76, "D" is the individual letter for the fourth aircraft in the *Staffel* and "A" represents the *Geschwaderstab*. The individual letter of staff aircraft would normally be painted Green or Blue. The combination of this *Geschwaderstab* identification with the Red markings is surprising, as Red markings are usually associated with II. *Gruppe*. These Red markings may therefore be the remnants of former service with KG(J) 54.

Although this aircraft is attached to a bomber unit, the external bomb racks are not fitted.

White outline type, and lower wing crosses are White outline with a Black center.

The tail *Hakenkreuz* appears to be solid Black, the fuselage *Balkenkreuz* is the The wings and horizontal tail planes are probably painted in a standard segmented scheme of 81 Brown-Violet/82 Bright Green. The leading edge of the wings displays a tight, wavy demarcation between upper and lower surfaces. Upper wing crosses are almost certainly the White outline style.

No. 7 Messerschmitt Me 262 V056
W. Nr. 170056

Werknummer 170056 was a flying test bed for elements of the proposed two-seater Me 262B-2a night fighter. The fin installed on the fuselage spine behind the cockpit was intended to assess the aerodynamic impact of the longer canopy required for the two-seater.

The aircraft is equipped with both FuG 218 *Neptun* radar on the nose, and FuG 226 vertical radar dipoles on the wings.

Werknummer 170056 was substantially repainted after initial testing of the *Neptun* radar. By war's end, the aircraft displayed large patches of a light color, possibly RLM 82 Bright Green, over its original Dark Green finish. A very dark color is also present on the mid fuselage near the rear of the canopy. Lower surfaces are painted RLM 76 Light Blue. A strip of bare metal can be seen between the steel nose and the alloy mid fuselage. The engine intake is also unpainted.

Although it is not visible in this view, the nose cap is painted a very dark color-probably RLM 70 Black-Green.

The *Hakenkreuz* is low-visibility White outline, as is the fuselage *Balkenkreuz*. The *werknummer* is stenciled in Black, and lower wing crosses are applied in Black and White.

No. 8 Messerschmitt Me 262,
W. Nr. 110506

Messerschmitt Me 262, W. Nr. 110506, as seen in northern Germany after discovery by Canadian forces. This aircraft is possibly finished in bomber colors RLM 65 Light Blue with a "squiggle" camouflage pattern of RLM 70 Black-Green and RLM 71 Dark Green on the upper surfaces of the wings and the fuselage. It is also possible that this low contrast scheme comprises the late-war colors 81 Brown-Violet and 83 Dark Green or even a combination of the old and new colors.

No. 9 Messerschmitt Me 262A-1a "Red 13"
(Located On Back Cover)

Obstl. Heinz Bär achieved 12 victories flying this Me 262 as *Kommandeur* of III./JG EJG 2. This aircraft may have been finished in upper surfaces of RLM 74 and RLM 75 Grays, or possibly RLM 82 Bright Green and RLM 83 Dark Green. The under surfaces were painted RLM 76 Light Blue. Bär's distinguishing individual aircraft number, "13" and the nose cap are Red.

Messerschmitt Me 262A-2a "Black X"
(Located On Back Cover)

Ofw. Hans-Robert Frölich flew this Me 262 A-2a to Hamburg on 8 May 1945; however the runway was obstructed so he flew on to Fassberg where he surrendered to the RAF and RCAF units occupying the airfield.

This bomber variant was equipped with the full complement of four 30 mm cannon.

His Stormbird was delivered with a Black and White *Hakenkreuz*, the *werknummer* stenciled on the fin and the last three digits, 200, hand-painted in Black on the nose. Photos of the same aircraft taken at Fassberg in May 1945, suggest that the *werknummer* and the "200" on the nose were later obscured with a field-applied camouflage touch up; and the White outline of the *Hakenkreuz* was painted out while "Black X" was in service.

The undersurfaces of this aircraft display variations in the shade of RLM 76 Bright Blue. The bomb racks are a paler Blue than the remainder of the lower nose. The lower rear fuselage and lower wings are unpainted metal with Dark Gray puttied panel lines. The engine nacelles are overall RLM 76 with the rear sections in heavily worn Black, possibly a temporary finish.

The upper surfaces feature thinly applied 81 Brown-Violet and 82 Bright Green. Dark Gray putty is visible along panel lines and 02 Gray can be seen under the thin camouflage colors. The nose cap and fin tip are painted RLM 23 Red.

The first intact Me 262 to be captured by American forces was W. Nr. 111711 delivered by the test pilot Hans Fay to Rhien-Main on 18 March 1945. Left in natural metal with only some stencil data, the panel lines are filled with a Gray putty, not the Yellow-Green as previously thought. Note, the lower portion of the rudder sheet metal stencil data printed on the lower portion of the rudder.

The nose of W. Nr. 111711 with American soldiers looking into the cockpit. Some Gray RLM 75 is evident on the nose cap.

After the war, many Me 262s were found in different stages of construction in open-air assembly stations along the München autobahn.

All line drawings courtesy Günther Sengfelder.

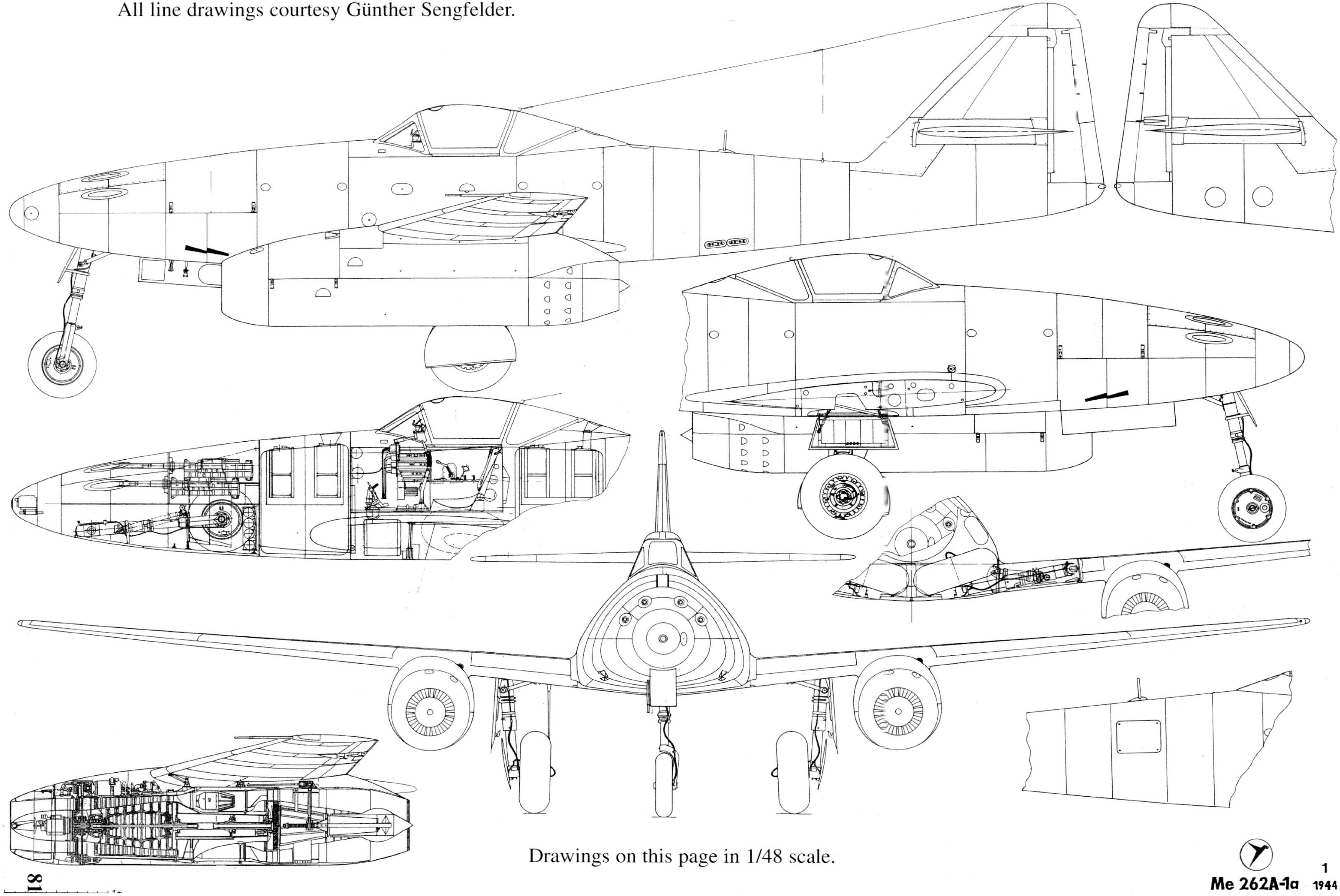

Drawings on this page in 1/48 scale.

Me 262A-1a 1944

1

81

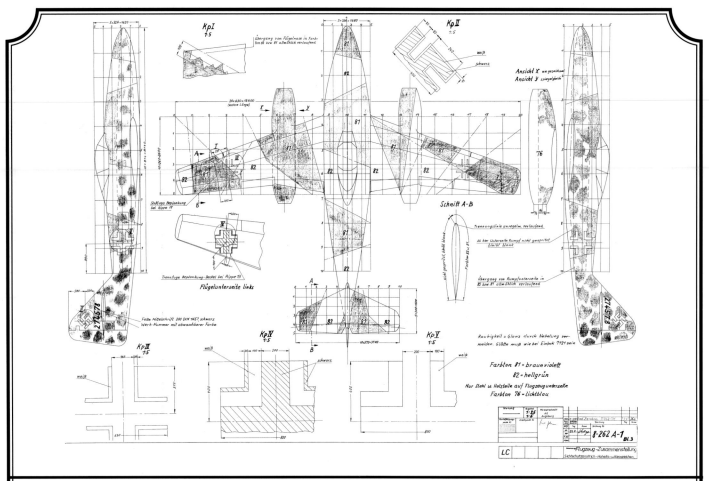

KpI 1:5

KpII 1:5

Ansicht X wie gezeichnet
Ansicht Y spiegelgleich

Schnitt A-B

Flügelunterseite links

KpIII 1:5

KpIV 1:5

KpV 1:5

Farbton 81 = braunviolett
82 = hellgrün
Nur Stahl u. Holzteile auf Flugzeugunterseite
Farbton 76 = Lichtblau

8-262 A-1 Bl.3

LC

Drawings on this page not to scale

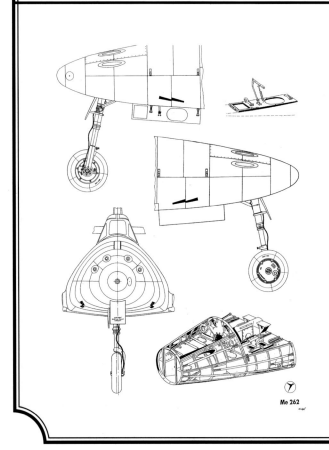

Me 262

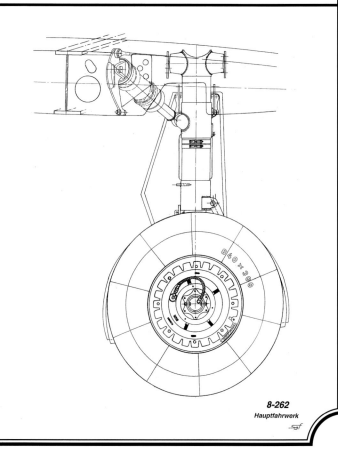

8-262
Hauptfahrwerk

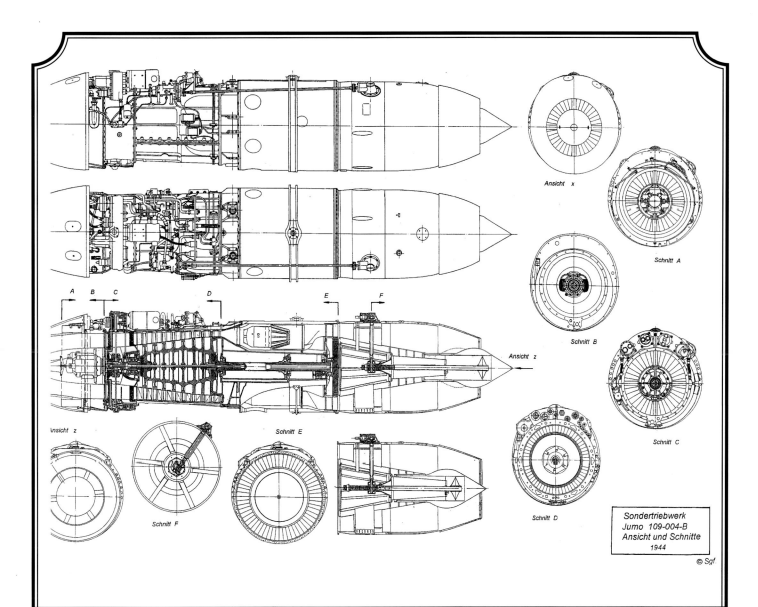

Ansicht x

Schnitt A

Schnitt B

Ansicht z

Schnitt C

Ansicht z

Schnitt E

Schnitt F

Schnitt D

A B C   D   E   F

Sondertriebwerk
Jumo 109-004-B
Ansicht und Schnitte
1944

© Sgf.

Drawings on this page not to scale

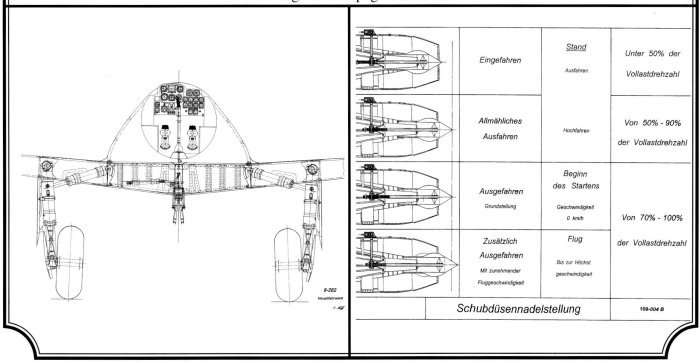

8-262
Hauptfahrwerk

	Eingefahren	Stand	Unter 50% der
		Ausfahren	Vollastdrehzahl
	Allmähliches Ausfahren	Hochfahren	Von 50% - 90% der Vollastdrehzahl
	Ausgefahren Grundstellung	Beginn des Startens Geschwindigkeit 0 km/h	Von 70% - 100% der Vollastdrehzahl
	Zusätzlich Ausgefahren Mit zunehmender Fluggeschwindigkeit	Flug Bis zur Höchst geschwindigkeit	
	Schubdüsennadelstellung		109-004 B

Werknummer
Data Plate Locations

From the official Messerschmitt document dated 10 May 1944, which
indicates data plate placement for the Me 262.

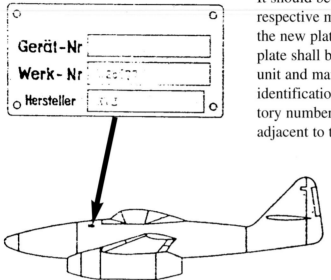

It should be noted that only the code identification of the respective manufacturer can be included. In the event that the new plates are not yet available, the formerly valid data plate shall be cut in the manner that the identification of unit and manufacturer is cut off. The manufacturer's code identification shall be entered in such cases behind the factory number. The acceptance seal shall be affixed directly adjacent to the data plate.

In the event that the respective airplane is intended for delivery at a company in a foreign country or in an occupied area or at a foreign office, respectively, the manufacturer shall not be identified in an overt or a coded form. The date plate shall be affixed at the left outer side of the body (see sketch).

Component Identification Manufacturing Regulations

III. Identification of the most important components by a "Component Data Plate"........ 16613

The identification of the required data shall be done according to the following example:

Item Number
Factory Number
Manufacturer

The following shall be noted:
1.) Item Number:
Identification of the drawing number with alteration letter.

2) Factory Number:
Identification of the factory number under which the group was manufactured with the running number within this group.

For the next group number, the running number begins again with 1.
Example: Comm. 13006, running number 6
On the component plate: 130065
Comm. 13006, running number 70
On the component plate: 1200670

3.) Manufacturer:
The manufacturer shall not be identified in overt nor coded form. The field designated for the manufacturer shall be empty.

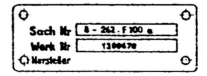

Component Data Plate Locations

Affixing these component data plates on the most important components at:
Fuselage
Fuselage tip
Tail unit carrier
Aileron
Horizontal Stabilizer - elevator
Vertical fin - rudder

Wing right and left
Landing gear inside - outside
Main wing inside – middle – outside

Vertical fin - rudder
Stabilizer
Rudder
Wing left – right

Drawings on this page in 1/48 scale.

Sonderbewaffnung 2x12 R 4 M

1m

References

Anon. 1995 *Dissolution of the Luftwaffe: the work of the British Air Forces of Occupation Germany* HMSO: London

Boehme, M. 1992 *JG 7: The World's First Jet Fighter Unit 1944/1945* Schiffer Publishing: Atglen PA

Boyne, W.J. 1994 *Messerschmitt Me 262: Arrow to the Future* Schiffer Publishing: Atglen PA

Brown, D.E. 1997 *Luftwaffe RLM Colors 81, 82 & 83 - A Commentary on their Evolution and Usage Parts 1, 2 and 3*, Experten Historical Aviation Research Inc., Bedford (published on the Internet in rec.models.scale newsgroup)

Brown, E. 1987 *Wings of the Luftwaffe: flying German aircraft of the Second World War* Airlife Publishing: Shrewbury

Butler, P. 1994 *War Prizes: an illustrated survey of German, Italian and Japanese aircraft brought to Allied countries during and after the Second World War* Midland Counties Publications: Leicester

Dierich, W. 1975 *Kampfgeschwader 'Edelweiss': the history of a German bomber unit 1939-1945* Ian Allan: London

Dressel, J and M. Griehl 1993 *Fighters of the Luftwaffe* Arms and Armour Press: London

Dressel, J and M. Griehl 1994 *Bombers of the Luftwaffe* Arms and Armour Press: London

Luftwaffe Color Chart 1999 published by Eagle Editions Ltd. Color chips supplied by German color company Warnecke & Böhm

Ethell, J and A. Price 1994 *World War II Fighting Jets* Airlife Publishing: Shrewsbury

Foreman, J. and S.E. Harvey 1995 *The Messerschmitt Me.262 Combat Diary* Second Edition Air Research Publications: Surrey

Forsyth, R. 1996 *JV 44: The Galland Circus* Classic Publications: West Sussex

Girbig, W. 1991 *Six Months to Oblivion: the defeat of the Luftwaffe fighter force over the Western Front 1944/1945* Schiffer Publishing: Atglen PA

Green, W. 1970 *Warplanes of the Third Reich* Macdonald and Jane's: London

Griehl, M. 1995 *Messerschmitt Me 262* The *Luftwaffe* Profile Series No. 1 Schiffer Publishing: Atglen PA

Griehl, M. 1992 *Messerschmitt Me 262: The World's First Turbojet Fighter* Vol. II Schiffer Publishing: Atglen PA

Heaton, J. 1983 "The Last Stormbird" *Journal of the Australian War Memorial* 2:24-33

Hecht, H. 1990 *The World's First Turbojet Fighter: Messerschmitt Me 262* Vol. I Schiffer Publishing: Atglen PA

Hess, W.N. 1996 *German Jets versus the U.S. Army Air Force* Specialty Press: Minnesota

Hildebrandt, C. 1993 *Broken Eagles 4: Me 262A* Fighter Pictorials: Perkiomenville, PA

Klaus, D.H. 1991 *IPMS Color Cross-Reference Guide*: published by the Author

McAuley, L. 1991 *Six Aces: Australian Fighter Pilots 1939-45* Banner Books: Melbourne

Merrick, K.A. 1977 *German Aircraft Markings 1939-1945* Sky Books Press: Great Britain

Merrick, K.A. 1968 *Messerschmitt Me 262 Described* Parts 1 and 2 Kookaburra Technical Publications Series 1: Dandenong

Merrick, K.A. and T.H. Hitchcock 1980 *The Official Monogram Painting Guide to German Aircraft 1935-1945* Monogram Aviation Publications: Massachusetts

Messerschmitt A.G. 1943 *Ersatzteil-Liste Me 262* Augsburg

Morgan, H. 1994 *Me 262: Stormbird Rising* Osprey Publishing: London

Oberkommando der *Luftwaffe* 1944 *Me 262 A-1, A-2 Flugzeug-Handbuch* Berlin

Radinger, W. and W. Schick 1993 *Messerschmitt Me 262: development, testing, production* Schiffer Publishing: Atglen PA

Rosch, B.C. 1995 *Luftwaffe Codes, Marking and Units 1939-1945* Schiffer Publishing: Atglen PA

Smith, J.R. and E.J. Creek 1983 *Monogram Close-Up 17: ME 262A-1* Monogram Aviation Publications: Boylston, Mass.

Smith, J.R. and E.J. Creek 1997 *Me 262 Volume One* Classic Publications: West Sussex

Smith, J.R. and E.J. Creek 1998 *Me 262 Volume Two* Classic Publications: West Sussex

Smith, J.R. and E.J. Creek 2000 *Me 262 Volume Three* Classic Publications: West Sussex

Smith, J.R. and E.J. Creek 2000 *Me 262 Volume Four* Classic Publications: West Sussex

Vajda, F.A. and Dancey, P.1998 *German Aircraft Industry and Production 1933-1945* Airlife: Shrewsbury

Addendum to
"𝕬𝖚𝖌𝖘𝖇𝖚𝖗𝖌'𝖘 𝕷𝖆𝖘𝖙 𝕰𝖆𝖌𝖑𝖊𝖘"

Here are two additional pictures of "Red 12", a Hungarian Messerschmitt Bf 109G-10 of Ung.J. St./101 that appeared on page 17 of EagleFiles EF#3 "Augsburg's Last Eagles". These views of the starboard side and the lower wing help complete the camouflage picture for this fascinating aircraft.

The lower wing is unpainted except for panel lines. These have been treated with a very pale color – probably RLM 76 Light Blue but possibly RLM 02 Gray. The lower control surfaces are finished in the same color. There appear to be no lower wing insignia on the star-

board wing. In the photo below, the overpainting of the fin Hakenkreuz is very apparent. Although the fuselage is painted RLM 75 Gray-Violet and RLM 83 Dark Green, the fin and rudder are a dark low contrast finish – probably RLM 81 Brown-Violet and RLM 83 Dark Green. Damage to the fuselage side below the cockpit has been patched and primed.

These two photographs were taken in the winter of 1945/46. The Messerschmitt Me 262 beneath "Red 12" is W. Nr. 500004.